Sampling and analysis

Enforcement

Legal proceedings

Appeals

Compensation and arbitration

Food Act 1984

CHAPTER 30

...ovisions of this consolida-
.. The Table has no official

SECTIONS

... of food

.. of injurious foods.
.. of food.

..ood etc.
..lars of ingredients.

..umption

..ted food.

..sing of vehicles
..tc.
..es.

A

Part VII

General and Supplemental

A 3

SCHEDULES:

Food Act 1984

1984 CHAPTER 30

An Act to consolidate the provisions of the Food and
Drugs Acts 1955 to 1982, the Sugar Act 1956, the Food
and Drugs (Milk) Act 1970, section 7(3) and (4) of the
European Communities Act 1972, section 198 of the
Local Government Act 1972 and Part IX of the Local
Government (Miscellaneous Provisions) Act 1982, and
connected provisions.   [26th June 1984]

BE IT ENACTED by the Queen's most Excellent Majesty, by and
with the advice and consent of the Lords Spiritual and
Temporal, and Commons, in this present Parliament
assembled, and by the authority of the same, as follows:—

PART I

FOOD GENERALLY

Composition and labelling of food

1.—(1) A person is guilty of an offence who—

   (a) adds any substance to food,

   (b) uses any substance as an ingredient in the preparation
      of food,

   (c) abstracts any constituent from food, or

   (d) subjects food to any other process or treatment,

Offences
as to
preparation
and sale of
injurious
foods.

A 4

so as (in any such case) to render the food injurious to health, with intent that the food shall be sold for human consumption in that state.

(2) A person is guilty of an offence who—

(a) sells for human consumption,

(b) offers, exposes or advertises for sale for human consumption, or has in his possession for the purpose of such sale,

any food rendered injurious to health by means of any operation described in subsection (1), subject to subsections (3) and (4).

(3) In proceedings under this section for an offence consisting of the advertisement for sale of any food, it is a defence for the person charged to prove that, being a person whose business it is to publish, or arrange for the publication of, advertisements, he received the advertisement for publication in the ordinary course of business.

(4) In determining for the purposes of this Act whether an article of food is injurious to health, regard shall be had not only to the probable effect of that article on the health of a person consuming it, but also to the probable cumulative effect of articles of substantially the same composition on the health of a person consuming such articles in ordinary quantities.

General protection for purchasers of food.

2.—(1) If a person sells to the purchaser's prejudice any food which is not—

(a) of the nature, or

(b) of the substance, or

(c) of the quality,

of the food demanded by the purchaser, he is guilty of an offence, subject to section 3.

(2) In subsection (1) the reference to sale shall be construed as a reference to sale for human consumption; and in proceedings under that subsection it is not a defence that the purchaser was not prejudiced because he bought for analysis or examination.

Defences in proceedings under s. 2.

3.—(1) In proceedings under section 2 for an offence consisting of the sale of food—

(a) to which any substance has been added, or

(b) in the preparation of which any substance has been used as an ingredient, or

(c) from which any constituent has been abstracted, or

(d) which has been subjected to any other process or treatment, other than food thereby rendered injurious to health, it is a defence to prove that—

(i) the operation in question was not carried out fraudulently, and

(ii) the article was sold with a notice attached to it of adequate size, distinctly and legibly printed and conspicuously visible, stating explicitly the nature of the operation, or was sold in a wrapper or container displaying such a notice.

(2) In proceedings under section 2 in respect of any food containing some extraneous matter, it is a defence to prove that the presence of that matter was an unavoidable consequence of the process of collection or preparation.

(3) In proceedings under section 2 in respect of diluted whisky, brandy, rum or gin, it is a defence to prove that—

(*a*) the spirit in question had been diluted with water only ; and

(*b*) its alcoholic strength by volume was still not lower than 37·2 per cent.

4.—(1) The Ministers may, so far as appears to them to be necessary or expedient in the interests of the public health, or otherwise for the protection of the public, or to be called for by any Community obligation, make regulations for any of the following purposes— Regulations as to composition of food etc.

(*a*) for requiring, prohibiting or regulating the addition of any specified substance, or any substance of any specified class, to food intended for sale for human consumption or any class of such food, or the use of any such substance as an ingredient in the preparation of such food, and generally for regulating the composition of such food ;

(*b*) for requiring, prohibiting or regulating the use of any process or treatment in the preparation of any food intended for sale for human consumption, or any class of such food ;

(*c*) for prohibiting or regulating the sale, possession for sale, offer or exposure for sale, consignment, or delivery, of food which does not comply with any of the regulations, or in relation to which an offence against the regulations has been committed or would have been committed if any relevant act or omission had taken place in England and Wales, or in Northern Ireland, subject to subsection (5), or for prohibiting or regulating the importation of any such food as is mentioned above ;

(*d*) for prohibiting or regulating the sale, possession for sale, or offer, exposure or advertisement for sale, of any specified substance, or of any substance of any specified class, with a view to its use in the preparation of food for human consumption, and the possesssion of any such substance for use in the preparation of food intended for sale for human consumption.

(2) In the exercise of their functions under this section the Ministers shall have regard to the desirability of restricting, so far as practicable, the use of substances of no nutritional value as foods or as ingredients of foods.

(3) Regulations made under this section may apply to cream, and to any food containing milk, but otherwise shall not apply to milk.

(4) Regulations so made may provide that, where any food is certified by a public analyst as being food to which the regulations apply so far as they are made under paragraph (*c*) of subsection (1), that food may be treated for the purposes of section 9, or in any corresponding Northern Ireland enactment, as being unfit for human consumption.

Those regulations may be—

(*a*) in relation to such cases as may be specified, and

(*b*) subject to such exceptions as may be allowed,

by or under the regulations, but nothing in any such regulations shall be taken as prejudicing the generality of the powers conferred by section 9, or in any corresponding Northern Ireland enactment.

(5) So far as this section relates to importation it applies to Northern Ireland.

Ministers'
power to
obtain
particulars of
ingredients.

5.—(1) To enable the Ministers to exercise their functions under section 4—

(*a*) they may by order require every person who at the date of the order or at any subsequent time carries on a business which includes the production, importation or use of substances of any class specified in the order to provide the Minister (within such time as may be so specified) with the particulars mentioned in paragraph (*b*);

(*b*) those particulars shall be such as may be so specified of the composition and use of any such substance sold in the course of that business for use in the preparation of food for human consumption, or used for that purpose in the course of that business.

(2) Without prejudice to the generality of subsection (1), an order made under that subsection may require the following particulars to be provided in respect of any substance—

(a) particulars of the composition and chemical formula of the substance;

(b) particulars of the manner in which the substance is used or proposed to be used in the preparation of food;

(c) particulars of any investigations carried out by or to the knowledge of the person carrying on the business in question, for the purpose of determining whether and to what extent the substance, or any product formed when the substance is used as mentioned above, is injurious to, or in any other way affects, health;

(d) particulars of any investigations or inquiries carried out by or to the knowledge of the person carrying on the business in question for the purpose of determining the cumulative effect on the health of a person consuming the substance in ordinary quantities.

(3) No particulars provided in accordance with an order under this section, and no information relating to any individual business obtained by means of such particulars, shall, without the previous consent in writing of the person carrying on the business in question, be disclosed except—

(a) in accordance with directions of the Minister, so far as may be necessary for the purposes of section 4 or of any corresponding enactment for the time being in force in Scotland or Northern Ireland,

(b) for the purposes of any proceedings for an offence against the order or any report of those proceedings,

and a person who discloses any such information or particulars in contravention of this subsection is guilty of an offence.

(4) Section 51 of the Patents Act 1949 (which secures inven- 1949 c. 87. tions against anticipation in certain cases) applies in relation—

(a) to the disclosure of any invention made in pursuance of an order under this section, and

(b) to anything done in consequence of any such disclosure,

as it applies in relation to such communications of inventions as are therein mentioned, and to anything done in consequence of such communications.

(5) So far as this section relates to importation it applies to Northern Ireland, and accordingly the words " production " and " or use " shall be omitted from subsection (1).

6.—(1) A person who gives with any food sold by him, or displays with any food exposed by him for sale, a label, whether or not attached to or printed on the wrapper or container, which—

    (*a*) falsely describes the food, or

    (*b*) is calculated to mislead as to its nature, or its substance or its quality,

is guilty of an offence, unless he proves that he did not know, and could not with reasonable diligence have ascertained, that the label was of such character as mentioned above.

(2) A person who publishes, or is a party to the publication of, an advertisement (not being such a label so given or displayed by him as mentioned above) which—

    (*a*) falsely describes any food, or

    (*b*) is calculated to mislead as to the nature, or the substance or the quality of any food,

is guilty of an offence, subject to subsection (3) ; and in any proceedings under this subsection against the manufacturer, producer or importer of the food, it rests on the defendant to prove that he did not publish, and was not a party to the publication of, the advertisement.

(3) In proceedings under subsection (2) it is a defence for the person charged to prove either—

    (*a*) that he did not know, and could not with reasonable diligence have ascertained, that the advertisement was of such a character as is described in that subsection, or

    (*b*) that, being a person whose business it is to publish, or arrange for the publication of, advertisements, he received the advertisement for publication in the ordinary course of business.

(4) For the purposes of this section, a label or advertisement which is calculated to mislead as to the nutritional or dietary value of any food is calculated to mislead as to the quality of the food.

(5) In proceedings for an offence under this section the fact that a label or advertisement in respect of which the offence is alleged to have been committed contained an accurate statement of the composition of the food shall not preclude the court from finding that the offence was committed.

(6) In this section references to sale shall be construed a. references to sale for human consumption.

7.—(1) The Ministers may make regulations for imposing requirements as to, and otherwise regulating—

    (*a*) the labelling, marking or advertising of food intended for sale for human consumption ; and

(b) the descriptions which may be applied to such food.

This provision is without prejudice to section 6.

(2) Regulations made under this section—

    (a) may apply to cream, and to any food containing milk (but shall not otherwise apply to milk) ;

    (b) may provide for any purpose authorised by paragraph (c) of section 4(1) in the case of regulations under that section.

(3) So far as this section relates to importation it applies to Northern Ireland.

Food unfit for human consumption

8.—(1) A person who—

    (a) sells, or offers or exposes for sale, or has in his possession for the purpose of sale or of preparation for sale, or

    (b) deposits with, or consigns to, any person for the purpose of sale or of preparation for sale,

any food intended for, but unfit for, human consumption is guilty of an offence, subject to subsection (3).

Sale etc. of unfit food.

(2) Where food in respect of which an offence under paragraph (a) of subsection (1) has been committed was sold to the offender by some other person, that person is also guilty of an offence, subject to subsection (3).

(3) Where a person is charged with an offence under paragraph (b) of subsection (1), or under subsection (2), it is a defence for him to prove either—

    (a) that he gave notice to the person with whom he deposited, or to whom he consigned or sold, the food in question that it was not intended for human consumption ; or

    (b) that, at the time when he delivered or despatched it to that person, either it was fit for human consumption or he did not know, and could not with reasonable diligence have ascertained, that it was unfit for human consumption.

(4) If a person licensed under section 1 of the Slaughterhouses Act 1974 to keep a slaughterhouse is convicted of an offence under this section, the court may cancel his licence, in addition to any other punishment.

1974 c. 3.

(5) The justice of the peace before whom any food is brought under section 9 may, but need not, be a member of the court

PART I

before which a person is charged with an offence under this section in relation to that food.

Examination and seizure of suspected food.

9.—(1) An authorised officer of a council—

    (*a*) may at all reasonable times examine any food intended for human consumption which has been sold, or is offered or exposed for sale, or is in the possession of, or has been deposited with or consigned to, any person for the purpose of sale or of preparation for sale ; and

    (*b*) if it appears to him to be unfit for human consumption, may seize it and remove it in order to have it dealt with by a justice of the peace.

(2) An officer who seizes any food under subsection (1) shall inform the person in whose possession the food was found of his intention to have it dealt with by a justice of the peace, and any person who under section 8 might be liable to a prosecution in respect of the food shall, if he attends before the justice of the peace upon the application for its condemnation, be entitled to be heard and to call witnesses.

(3) If it appears to a justice of the peace that any food brought before him, whether seized under the provisions of this section or not, is unfit for human consumption, he shall condemn it and order it to be destroyed or to be so disposed of as to prevent it from being used for human consumption.

(4) If a justice of the peace refuses to condemn any food seized under this Part by an authorised officer of a council, the council shall compensate the owner of the food for any depreciation in its value resulting from its seizure and removal.

Food as prizes etc.

10. Sections 8 and 9 apply—

    (*a*) in relation to any food which is intended for human consumption and is offered as a prize or reward in connection with any entertainment to which the public are admitted, whether on payment of money or not, as if the food were, or had been, exposed for sale by each person concerned in the organisation of the entertainment ;

    (*b*) in relation to any food which is intended for human consumption and is offered as a prize or reward or given away for the purpose of advertisement, or in furtherance of any trade or business, as if the food were, or had been, exposed for sale by the person offering or giving away the food ; and

(c) in relation to any food which is intended for human consumption and is exposed or deposited in any premises for the purpose of being so offered or given away as mentioned above, as if the food were, or had been, exposed for sale by the occupier of the premises.

In this section " entertainment " includes any social gathering, amusement, exhibition, performance, game, sport or trial of skill.

11.—(1) If an authorised officer of a council has reason to suspect that any vehicle or container contains any food—

(a) which is intended for sale for human consumption, or

(b) which is in the course of delivery after sale for human consumption,

he may examine the contents of the vehicle or container, subject to subsections (4) and (5).

(2) For that purpose the officer may, if necessary, detain the vehicle or container.

(3) If the officer finds any food which appears to him to be intended for, but unfit for, human consumption, he may deal with it as food falling within section 9(1), and subsections (2) to (4) of that section shall apply accordingly.

(4) Nothing in this section authorises the detention of—

(a) any vehicle belonging to any of the Boards established by the Transport Act 1962, the London Transport Executive, and their wholly owned subsidiaries, and used by them for the purposes of any railway operated by them ;

1962 c. 46.

(b) any vehicle belonging to a railway company and used by them for the purposes of their undertaking ;

(c) any authorised vehicle used for the purpose of his business as a carrier of goods by a person holding a licence under Part V of the Transport Act 1968.

1968 c. 73.

(5) Where the duties of an officer of customs and excise with respect to any goods have not been wholly discharged, nothing in this section authorises the examination of those goods without his consent.

12.—(1) No person shall, for human consumption—

(a) sell, or

(b) offer or expose for sale, or

(c) have in his possession for the purpose of sale or of preparation for sale,

PART I   any part of, or product derived wholly or partly from, an animal which has been slaughtered in a knacker's yard or of which the carcase has been brought into a knacker's yard.

(2) A person who contravenes subsection (1) is guilty of an offence, and, if he is licensed under section 1 of the Slaughter-houses Act 1974 to keep either a slaughterhouse or a knacker's yard, the court may, in addition to any other punishment, cancel his licence.

1974 c. 3.

Hygiene

Regulations as to food hygiene.

13.—(1) The Ministers may make such regulations as appear to them to be expedient for securing the observance of sanitary and cleanly conditions and practices in connection with—

(a) the sale of food for human consumption, or

(b) the importation, preparation, transport, storage, packaging, wrapping, exposure for sale, service or delivery of food intended for sale or sold for human consumption,

or otherwise for the protection of the public health in connection with those matters.

(2) Without prejudice to the generality of subsection (1), regulations made under this section may provide—

(a) for imposing requirements as to the construction, layout, drainage, equipment, maintenance, cleanliness, ventilation, lighting, water-supply and use of premises in, at or from which food is sold for human consumption, or offered, exposed, stored or prepared for sale, for human consumption (including any parts of such premises in which apparatus and utensils are cleansed, or in which refuse is disposed of or stored);

(b) for imposing requirements as to the provision, maintenance and cleanliness of sanitary and washing facilities in connection with such premises, the disposal of refuse and the maintenance and cleanliness of apparatus, equipment, furnishings and utensils used in such premises, and in particular for imposing requirements that every sanitary convenience situated in such premises shall be supplied with water through a suitable flushing appliance;

(c) for prohibiting or regulating the use of any specified materials, or of materials of any specified class, in the manufacture of apparatus or utensils designed for use in the preparation of food for human consumption, and the sale or importation for sale of apparatus or utensils designed for such use and containing any specified materials, or materials of any specified class;

(d) for prohibiting spitting on premises where food is sold for human consumption, or offered, exposed, stored or prepared for sale for human consumption (including any parts of such premises where apparatus and utensils are cleansed):

(e) for imposing requirements as to the clothing worn by persons in such premises;

(f) for securing the inspection of animals intended for slaughter, and of carcases of animals, for the purpose of ascertaining whether meat intended for sale for human consumption is fit for such consumption;

(g) for requiring the staining or sterilisation in accordance with the regulations of meat which is unfit for human consumption, or which is derived from animals slaughtered in knackers' yards or from carcases brought into knackers' yards, or which, though not unfit for human consumption, is not intended for such consumption;

(h) for regulating generally the treatment and disposal of any food unfit for human consumption;

(j) for prohibiting or regulating, or enabling local authorities to prohibit or regulate, the sale for human consumption, or the offer, exposure or distribution for sale for human consumption, of shellfish taken from beds or other layings for the time being designated by or under the regulations.

In this subsection "animals" includes poultry.

(3) Regulations under this section may make different provisions in relation to different classes of business; and, without prejudice to the foregoing provisions of this section or section 118, any such regulations imposing requirements in respect of premises may—

(a) impose on the occupier of the premises and, in the case of requirements of a structural character, on any owner of the premises who either lets them for use for a purpose to which the regulations apply or permits them to be so used after notice from the authority charged with the enforcement of the regulations, responsibility for compliance with those requirements;

(b) provide, subject to such limitations and safeguards as may be specified, for conferring, in relation to particular premises, exemptions from the operation of specified provisions contained in regulations made for the purposes of paragraph (a) or paragraph (b) of subsection (2) while there is in force a certificate of the local authority to the effect that compliance with those provisions cannot reasonably be required with respect to the premises or any activities carried on in them.

(4) If any person who has incurred, or is about to incur, expenditure in securing that the requirements of regulations made under this section, being requirements of a structural character, are complied with in respect of any premises owned or occupied by him claims that the whole or any part of the expenditure ought to be borne by any other person having an interest in the premises, he may apply to the county court.

(5) The court may make such order concerning the expenditure or its apportionment as appears to the court, having regard to all the circumstances of the case, including the terms of any contract between the parties, to be just and equitable ; and any order made under this subsection may direct that any such contract as mentioned above shall cease to have effect in so far as it is inconsistent with the terms of the order.

(6) Regulations made under this section may impose in respect of accommodation in home-going ships, and in respect of vehicles, stalls and places other than premises, any such requirements as may be imposed under the regulations in respect of premises.

(7) References in this section to food shall be construed as references to food other than milk, except that—

> (a) regulations under this section relating to importation may apply to milk ; and

> (b) any regulations under this section may apply to any food containing milk.

(8) The Ministers shall from time to time take such steps as they think expedient for publishing codes of practice in connection with matters which may be made the subject of regulations under this section, for the purpose of giving advice and guidance to persons responsible for compliance with such regulations.

(9) If a person convicted of an offence against any regulations made under this section with respect to slaughterhouses or knackers' yards is the holder of a licence under section 1 of the Slaughterhouses Act 1974 in respect of the premises where the offence was committed, the court may, in addition to any other punishment, cancel the licence.

1974 c. 3.

(10) So far as this section relates to importation it applies to Northern Ireland.

14.—(1) The provisions of this section have effect where a
person is proceeded against by a local authority for an offence against regulations made under section 13 in respect—

    (*a*) of any premises used as catering premises ; or

    (*b*) of any business carried on at such premises.

(2) If the person is convicted of the offence and the court thinks it expedient to do so—

    (*a*) having regard to the gravity of the offence or (in the case of an offence committed in respect of premises) to the unsatisfactory nature of the premises, or

    (*b*) having regard to any offences against regulations made under section 13 of which the person has been previously convicted,

the court may, on the application of the local authority, make an order disqualifying that person from using those premises as catering premises for such period not exceeding 2 years as may be specified in the order.

(3) An order under this section shall not be made against any person unless the local authority have, not less than 14 days before the date of the hearing, given that person written notice of their intention to apply for an order to be made against him.

(4) A person subject to an order under this section is guilty of an offence if, while the order is in force—

    (*a*) he uses the premises to which the order relates as catering premises ; or

    (*b*) he participates in the management of any business in the course of which the premises are so used by another person.

(5) A person so subject may, from time to time after the expiry of 6 months from the date on which the order came into force, apply to the court before which he was convicted, or by which the order was made, to revoke the order ; but where such an application is refused by the court a further application under this subsection shall not be entertained if made within 3 months of the refusal.

(6) On any such application the court may, if it thinks proper having regard to all the circumstances of the case, including in particular—

    (*a*) the person's conduct subsequent to the conviction, and

    (*b*) any improvement in the state of the premises to which the order relates,

grant the application.

(7) The court to which an application under subsection (5) is made has power to order the applicant to pay the whole or any part of the costs of the application.

Byelaws as to food.
15. A local authority may make byelaws for securing the observance of sanitary and cleanly conditions and practices—

(a) in connection with the handling, wrapping and delivery of food sold or intended for sale for human consumption ; and

(b) in connection with the sale or exposure for sale in the open air of food intended for human consumption.

Registration of premises and licensing of vehicles

Registration: ice-cream, sausages etc.
16.—(1) No premises shall be used for—

(a) the sale, or the manufacture for the purpose of sale, of ice-cream, or the storage of ice-cream intended for sale, or

(b) the preparation or manufacture of sausages or potted, pressed, pickled or preserved food intended for sale,

unless they are registered under this section for that purpose by the local authority.

For the purposes of this subsection—

(i) " sale " means sale for human consumption ;

(ii) the preparation of meat or fish by any process of cooking shall be deemed to be the preservation of that meat or fish.

(2) A person who uses any premises in contravention of subsection (1) is guilty of an offence.

(3) Nothing in this Part applies so as to require the registration under this section—

(a) of premises used wholly or mainly as catering premises, or

(b) of premises used wholly or mainly as a school or club, or

(c) of domestic premises, if the only food intended for sale which is prepared or manufactured on them is food intended for sale for the benefit of the person preparing or manufacturing it by a society registered under the Industrial and Provident Societies Act 1965, or

1965 c. 12.

(d) of premises of any description, if the only food intended for sale which is prepared or manufactured on them is food prepared or manufactured otherwise than in the course of a trade carried on by the person preparing or manufacturing it, and paragraph (*a*) of subsection (1) does not apply in relation to the sale or storage of ice-cream at any premises used as a theatre, cinematographic theatre, music hall or concert hall.

(4) This section does not apply in relation to premises—

(*a*) which are used for the preparation, sale or storage of articles prepared from, or consisting of, materials other than those of animal or vegetable origin, but

(*b*) which are not otherwise used for any purpose in connection with the preparation, storage or sale of food,

except so far as may be expressly provided by regulations made under this Part.

(5) Where in any district—

(*a*) local Act provisions were in force at the commencement of this Act with respect to the registration of premises used for any of the purposes mentioned in subsection (1), and

(*b*) those provisions were in force at the commencement of the Food and Drugs Act 1938 (1st October 1939), 1938 c. 56.

that subsection, so far as it relates to registration for purposes regulated by the local Act provisions, shall not apply to that district until the Secretary of State, on the local authority's application, declares it to be in force there.

(6) Where on an application made by a local authority under subsection (5) the Secretary of State declares subsection (1) to be in force in the authority's district, then, upon the declaration taking effect, such of the local Act provisions referred to in subsection (5) as may be specified in the declaration shall be repealed, or, as the case may be, shall be repealed as respects the authority's district.

(7) Any premises which immediately before the repeal of those provisions were registered under them for any purpose mentioned in subsection (1) shall be deemed to have been registered under this section for the purpose in question.

17.—(1) The Ministers may by order direct that section 16 shall have effect as if the purposes described in subsection (1) of that section included, except in such cases as may be prescribed by the order—

(*a*) the sale or preparation for sale of food for human consumption, or

(*b*) the storage of food intended for such sale,

in the course of any business of a class specified in the order.

(2) An order made under this section shall provide—

(*a*) for enabling premises used for purposes for which registration is required by the order to be registered under section 16 before the date when subsection (1) of that section becomes applicable to them by the order : and

(b) in relation to premises used for those purposes before that date, for excluding or restricting the power of the local authority to refuse applications for registration.

(3) The purposes for which registration is required by an order made under this section may include any purpose for which, apart from the order, registration would be required under section 16.

(4) Any such order—

(a) may repeal, in whole or in part, paragraph (a) or (b) of section 16(1) ; and

(b) may provide for continuing in force the registration of any premises for purposes to which the order applies.

(5) If—

(a) at the time when premises become registrable for any purposes by an order made under this section, local Act provisions with respect to the registration of premises used for any of those purposes are in force in any district, then

(b) section 16(1), as having effect by the order, shall not, so far as it relates to registration for purposes regulated by the local Act provisions, apply to that district until the Secretary of State, on the application of the local authority, declares it to be in force there.

(6) Where on an application made by a local authority under subsection (5) the Secretary of State declares section 16(1) to be in force in the authority's district, then, upon the declaration taking effect, such of the local Act provisions referred to in subsection (5) as may be specified in the declaration shall be repealed or, as the case may be, shall be repealed as respects the authority's district.

(7) Any premises which immediately before the repeal of those provisions were registered under them for any of the purposes for which premises become registrable by virtue of the relevant order made under this section shall be deemed to have been registered under section 16 for the purpose in question.

Application for registration.

18.—(1) An application for the registration of any premises under section 16 shall specify—

(a) the purpose or purposes for which the registration is applied for, and

(b) all rooms or accommodation in the premises proposed to be used for those purposes, and on such an application being made as mentioned above by the occupier of, or a person proposing to occupy, the premises to which the application relates, the local authority shall, subject to this section and section 19, register the premises for those purposes.

(2) The local authority—

   (*a*) may register the same premises for more than one purpose for which registration under section 16 is required ; and

   (*b*) may register different parts of the same premises for different purposes.

(3) The premises registered under section 16 in pursuance of such an application as is mentioned above shall not include any room or accommodation not specified in the application.

(4) Upon any change in the occupation of premises registered under section 16, the incoming occupier shall, if he intends to use them for the purpose for which they are registered, forthwith give notice of the change to the local authority, who shall thereupon make any necessary alteration in their register.

If a person required to give a notice under this subsection fails to do so, he shall be liable to a fine not exceeding level 1 on the standard scale.

19.—(1) Subsection (2) applies in the case of any premises Refusal or in respect of which an application is made for registration under cancellation of section 16, or which are registered under that section, if it registration. appears to the local authority—

   (*a*) that the requirements of regulations in force under section 13 are not complied with in connection with the premises or the business carried on at the premises ; or

   (*b*) that the premises or any part of the premises are otherwise unsuitable (having regard to considerations of hygiene and in particular to the situation, construction or condition of the premises, or to any activities carried on in them) for use for the purpose or purposes specified in the application, or for which they are used, as the case may be.

(2) In such a case the authority may serve on the applicant for registration or, as the case may be, on the occupier of the premises, a notice—

   (*a*) stating the place and time (not being less than 21 days after the date of the service of the notice) at which they propose to take the matter into consideration ; and

(b) informing him that he may there and then attend before them, with any witnesses whom he desires to call, to show cause why the authority should not, for reasons specified in the notice. refuse the application or, as the case may be, cancel the registration of the premises.

(3) A person entitled under subsection (2) to appear before any authority—

(a) may appear in person or by counsel or a solicitor or any other representative ; or

(b) may be accompanied by any person whom he may wish to assist him in the proceedings.

(4) If a person on whom a notice is served under subsection (2) fails to show cause to the local authority's satisfaction, they may refuse the application or, as the case may be, cancel the registration of the premises, and

(a) shall forthwith give notice to him of their decision in the matter ; and

(b) shall, if so required by him within 14 days from the date of their decision, give to him, not later than 48 hours after receiving the requirement, a statement of the grounds of the decision.

(5) A person aggrieved by the decision of a local authority under this section to refuse to register any premises, or to cancel the registration of any premises, may appeal to a magistrates' court.

Regulations for licensing vehicles, stalls etc.

20.—(1) The Ministers may make regulations providing—

(a) for the issue by local authorities of licences in respect of the use of vehicles, stalls or places other than premises, for the preparation, exposure or offer for sale, or sale, of food for human consumption ; and

(b) for prohibiting the use for any such purpose of any such vehicle, stall or place except in accordance with a licence issued under the regulations.

(2) Regulations under this section—

(a) may be made so as to apply either generally or to such class or classes of businesses as may be specified in the regulations ; and

(b) may exempt from the requirements of this Act as to registration under section 16 any premises used for the storage of food intended for sale for human consumption in the course of a business in respect of which a licence is in force under the regulations.

(3) Regulations made under this section may provide for the refusal or cancellation of a licence under the regulations, either

wholly or in respect of a part of the business for which the PART I licence is applied for or is held—

> (a) where the requirements of regulations in force under section 13 are not complied with in relation to that business, or
>
> (b) where the applicant or holder is unable or has failed to comply, in relation to that business, with any byelaws in force under section 15,

and such regulations shall provide for affording to persons affected by any such refusal or cancellation an opportunity to make representations to the local authority, and to appeal from that authority's decision to a magistrates' court.

(4) Where—

> (a) any regulations under this section in relation to any class of business come into operation, and
>
> (b) local Act provisions are then in force in any district, being provisions under which persons engaged in that class of business are required to be licensed or registered,

the regulations so far as they relate to that class of business shall not apply to that district until such date as may be appointed by an order made by the Secretary of State upon the local authority's application in that behalf.

(5) Where an order is made under subsection (4) in relation to any district, that order—

> (a) may repeal any such local Act provisions as are mentioned in that subsection, so far as they relate to that district and to the class of business in relation to which the regulations under this section have effect ; and
>
> (b) shall provide for securing that persons licensed or registered under those provisions are, in relation to any business of that class in which they are engaged, treated as licensed under the regulations.

Control of food premises

21.—(1) Where on an information laid by a local authority a Closure order. person is convicted of an offence under regulations made under section 13 and the offence includes—

> (a) the carrying on of a food business at any insanitary premises or at any premises the condition, situation or construction of which is such that food is exposed to the risk of contamination, or
>
> (b) the carrying on of a food business on, at or from a stall which is insanitary, or which is so situated or con-

structed, or is in such a condition, that the food is exposed to the risk of contamination,

then, subject to subsection (2), if the court is satisfied that—

(i) food continues or is likely to continue to be prepared, stored, sold or offered or exposed for sale at those premises or on, at or from that stall, and

(ii) by reason of the situation, construction or insanitary or defective condition of the premises or stall or the insanitary or defective condition of the fittings or fixtures or equipment or the infestation of vermin or the accumulation of refuse, the carrying on of a food business at those premises or on, at or from that stall would be dangerous to health,

the court may on the local authority's application, whether or not it makes any other order, by order (called " a closure order ") prohibit the preparation, storage, sale or offer or exposure for sale at those premises or on, at or from that stall of food until the local authority certifies under subsection (4) that such specified measures as the court considers necessary to remove the danger to health have been carried out.

(2) A closure order shall not be made unless the local authority have, not less than 14 days before the trial of the information, given—

(a) the person against whom the information was laid, and

(b) if he is not that person, the owner of the premises or stall (unless the local authority are unable after reasonable inquiry to ascertain his identity),

written notice of their intention to apply for the order.

(3) The local authority shall in any notice under subsection (2) specify the measures which, in their opinion, should be taken to remove any danger to health.

(4) Any person who wishes to carry on a food business at any premises or on, at or from any stall with respect to which a closure order is in force may apply to the local authority who, if satisfied that the measures specified by the closure order have been carried out, shall as soon as practicable and in not more than 14 days give to the applicant a certificate to that effect, and such certificate shall be conclusive evidence of the matters stated in it.

Emergency order.

22.—(1) Where an information is, or has been, laid by a local authority in relation to an offence described in section 21(1) and application is made by the local authority for an order under this section, the court may, subject to subsection (2), if satisfied—

   (*a*) by evidence tendered by the local authority, and

   (*b*) after affording, if he appears, the person against whom the information is or was laid and, if he is not that person, the owner of the premises or stall, an opportunity to be heard and tender evidence,

that the use of the premises or stall for the preparation, storage, sale or offer or exposure for sale of food involves imminent risk of danger to health, make an order (called " an emergency order ") prohibiting, either absolutely or subject to conditions, the use of those premises or that stall for those purposes until—

   (i) the determination of the proceedings to which the information gave rise, or

   (ii) the issue of a certificate by the local authority under subsection (6),

whichever is the earlier.

(2) The court shall not consider an application under this section unless it is satisfied that at least three clear days' notice in writing of intention to make that application and of the time at which it would be made has been given to the person against whom the information is or was laid and, if he is not that person, to the owner of the premises or stall.

(3) The local authority shall in any notice under subsection (2) specify the measures which, in their opinion, should be taken to remove any danger to health.

(4) Notice for the purpose of subsection (2) may be served in any way, except by post, authorised by rules made under section 144 of the Magistrates' Courts Act 1980 for the service of 1980 c. 43. a summons issued by a justice of the peace or by leaving it for him with some person who appears to be employed at the premises or stall to which the information relates.

(5) The local authority shall serve a copy of an emergency order made under this section as soon as may be after the order has been made on the person against whom the information was laid and, if he is not that person, on the owner of the premises or stall, and shall affix a copy of it in a conspicuous position on the premises or, if practicable, on the stall.

(6) Any person who wishes to carry on a food business at any premises or on, at or from any stall, with respect to which an emergency order is in force, may apply to the local authority who, if satisfied there is no longer any risk of danger to health, shall as soon as practicable and in not more than 14 days issue a certificate to that effect.

23.—(1) If on the trial of an information relating to an offence described in section 21(1) the court, on the application of an interested person—

(a) determines that at the date of any emergency order the use of the premises or stall did not involve imminent risk of danger to health, and

(b) is satisfied that loss has been occasioned by the emergency order,

the court may order the local authority to pay to that person compensation of such amount as the court thinks proper.

(2) The following are interested persons for the purposes of subsection (1) and section 24(2)—

(a) the person against whom the information was laid ;

(b) the owner of the premises or stall ;

(c) any person not within paragraph (a) or (b) who at the time when the emergency order was made was carrying on a food business at those premises or on, at or from that stall.

24.—(1) Where an application for a closure order is refused or granted—

(a) if the application is refused, the local authority who made the application may appeal to the Crown Court ;

(b) if the application is granted, any person to whom notice of the application was given under section 21(2) may appeal as mentioned in paragraph (a).

(2) Where an application for an order under section 23 for the payment of compensation is granted or refused, the following persons may appeal to the Crown Court—

(a) the local authority who made the application for the emergency order in question ; or

(b) any interested person who applied for the payment of compensation under that section in respect of that order.

(3) Where a person applies for a certificate under section 21(4) or 22(6), and the local authority refuses or fails to give it, the applicant may appeal to a magistrates' court who may, if satisfied that it is proper to do so, direct the authority to give such certificate.

25.—(1) A person who contravenes a closure order or an emergency order is liable on summary conviction to a fine not ex- Offences ceeding level 5 on the standard scale. against food premises

(2) In the application of the provisions of sections 21, 22, 23 control. and 24, and of subsection (1) of this section, in connection with an offence under any such regulations as are mentioned in section 21(1)—

> (*a*) any expression to which a meaning is given by the regulations in question shall, unless the context otherwise requires, have the same meaning in those provisions as in those regulations ; and
>
> (*b*) those provisions shall have effect as if the references to premises included places which are not premises within the meaning of those regulations.

26. In relation to any offence under regulations made under Ships. section 13 which includes the carrying on of a food business—

> (*a*) in any insanitary ship, or
>
> (*b*) in any ship the condition, situation or construction of which is such that food is exposed to the risk of contamination,

the Secretary of State may make regulations containing provisions corresponding to those of sections 21, 22, 23, 24 and 25, with such additions, omissions or other modifications as he thinks fit.

As to regulations under this section—

> (i) the penalty provided by any provision of such regulations which corresponds to section 25(1) shall be the same as in that subsection ;
>
> (ii) the only provision of Parts VI and VII which applies to the exercise of the power to make such regulations is section 120.

Ice-cream, horseflesh and shellfish

27.—(1) Every dealer in ice-cream who in a street or other Sale of place of public resort sells, or offers or exposes for sale, ice- ice-cream cream— from stalls etc.

> (*a*) from a stall or vehicle, or
>
> (*b*) from a container used without a stall or vehicle,

shall have his name and address legibly and conspicuously displayed on the stall, vehicle or container, as the case may be, and, if he fails to comply with the requirements of this section, shall be liable to a fine not exceeding level 1 on the standard scale.

(2) A local authority may at any time resolve that, as from such date, not being less than 4 weeks from the date of the passing of the resolution, as may be there specified and until the resolution is revoked, this section shall apply within their district in relation—

(a) to all kinds of food, or

(b) to any kinds of food specified in the resolution,

as it applies in relation to ice-cream, and while any such resolution is in force this section shall apply accordingly.

Nothing in this subsection has effect in relation to milk.

(3) A local authority shall forthwith give notice to the Secretary of State of the passing or revocation of a resolution under this section and shall take such steps as he may direct for publishing notice of the coming into operation, or revocation, of any such resolution.

Prevention of spread of disease by ice-cream.

28.—(1) Every manufacturer of, or dealer in, ice-cream shall, upon the occurrence of any disease to which this subsection applies among the persons living or working in or about the premises on which the ice-cream is manufactured, stored or sold, forthwith give notice of the occurrence to the local authority for the district and, if he fails to do so, shall be liable to a fine not exceeding level 1 on the standard scale.

(2) Subsection (1) applies to the diseases specified in Schedule 1 and any other disease which the Secretary of State may by order declare to be a disease to which that subsection applies.

(3) If the proper officer of a local authority has reasonable ground for suspecting that any ice-cream, or substance intended for use in the manufacture of ice-cream, is likely to cause any disease communicable to human beings, he may give notice to the person in charge of it that, until further notice, the ice-cream or substance in question, or any specified portion of it, is not to be used for human consumption and either—

(a) is not to be removed ; or

(b) is not to be removed except to some place specified in the notice.

A person who uses or removes any ice-cream or substance in contravention of the requirements of a notice given under this subsection shall be liable to a fine not exceeding level 5 on the standard scale.

(4) If on further investigation the proper officer of the local authority is satisfied that the ice-cream or substance in question may safely be used for human consumption, he shall forthwith withdraw his notice ; but, if he is not so satisfied—

(a) he shall cause it to be destroyed, and

(*b*) he shall also cause to be destroyed any other ice-cream or such substance as mentioned above then on the premises as to which he is not so satisfied.

(5) Where a notice given under subsection (3) is withdrawn by the proper officer of the local authority, or the proper officer acting under subsection (4) causes any ice-cream or other substance to be destroyed, the local authority shall compensate the owner of the ice-cream or other substance in question for any depreciation in its value resulting from the action taken by the proper officer or, as the case may be, for the loss of its value.

(6) As to compensation under this section—

(*a*) no compensation shall be payable in respect of the destruction of any ice-cream or substance if the local authority prove that it was likely to cause any disease communicable to human beings;

(*b*) no compensation shall in any case be payable—

(i) in respect of any ice-cream or substance manufactured on, or brought within, any premises while a notice given under subsection (3) with respect to anything on those premises was operative, or

(ii) in any case where the owner of the ice-cream or substance in question has failed to give a notice which he was required by subsection (1) to give.

For the purposes of this subsection, the value of any ice-cream or other substance shall not be assessed at a sum exceeding the cost incurred by the owner in making or purchasing it.

29.—(1) A person is guilty of an offence who— Sale of horseflesh.

(*a*) sells, or

(*b*) offers or exposes for sale, or

(*c*) has in his possession for the purpose of sale,

any horseflesh for human consumption elsewhere than—

(i) in premises, or

(ii) in a stall, vehicle or place,

over or on which a notice in legible letters stating that horseflesh is sold there is displayed in a conspicuous position so as to be visible whenever horseflesh is being sold, or offered or exposed for sale.

(2) A person is guilty of an offence who supplies horseflesh for human consumption to a purchaser—

(*a*) who has not asked to be supplied with horseflesh; or

(*b*) who has asked to be supplied with some compound article of food not ordinarily made of horseflesh.

(3) If any horseflesh is exposed for sale elsewhere than in premises, or in a stall, vehicle or place, distinguished as mentioned above without anything to show that it was not intended for sale for human consumption, the onus of proving that it was not so intended shall rest upon the person exposing it for sale.

(4) In this section " horseflesh " means the flesh of horses, asses and mules, and includes any such flesh—

(a) whether cooked or uncooked, and

(b) whether alone, or accompanied by, or mixed with, any other substance,

and " flesh " includes any part of any such animal.

Cleansing of shellfish.

30.—(1) A county council or a local authority—

(a) may provide, whether within or without their county or district, tanks or other apparatus for cleansing shellfish ; and

(b) may make charges in respect of the use of any tank or other apparatus so provided.

(2) A county council or a local authority may contribute towards the expenses incurred under this section by any other council or any joint committee, or towards expenses incurred by any other person in providing, and making available to the public, means for cleansing shellfish.

(3) Any expenses incurred by a county council under this section shall, if the Secretary of State by order so directs, be defrayed as expenses for special county purposes chargeable upon such part of the county as may be provided by the order.

(4) In this section " cleansing shellfish " includes the subjection of shellfish to any germicidal treatment.

(5) Nothing in this section authorises the establishment of any tank or other apparatus, or the execution of any other work, on, over or under tidal lands below high-water mark of ordinary spring tides, except in accordance with such plans and sections, and subject to such restrictions and conditions as may before the work is commenced be approved by the Secretary of State.

Food poisoning

Inspection and control of infected food.

31.—(1) If the proper officer of a local authority has reasonable ground for suspecting that any food of which he, or any other officer of the local authority of the district, has procured a sample under the provisions of this Act is likely to cause food poisoning, he may give notice to the person in charge of the food that, until his investigations are completed—

(a) the food, or any specified portion of it, is not to be used for human consumption, and (*b*) either is not to be removed, or is not to be removed except to some place specified in the notice.

A person who uses or removes any food in contravention of the requirements of a notice given under this subsection is liable to a fine not exceeding level 5 on the standard scale.

(2) If, as a result of his investigations, the proper officer is satisfied that the food in question, or any portion of it, is likely to cause food poisoning, he may deal with it as food falling within section 9(1) and subsections (2) and (3) of that section shall apply accordingly; but, if he is satisfied that it may be safely used for human consumption, he shall forthwith withdraw his notice.

(3) If a notice given under subsection (1) is withdrawn by the proper officer, or if the justice of the peace before whom any food is brought under this section refuses to condemn it, the local authority shall compensate the owner of the food to which the notice related for any depreciation in its value resulting from the action taken by the proper officer.

PART II

MILK, DAIRIES AND CREAM SUBSTITUTES

Milk and dairies

32.—(1) In the following provisions of this Act—

(*a*) " dairy "—

(i) includes any farm, cowshed, milking house, milk store, milk shop or other premises from which milk is supplied on or for sale, or in which milk is kept or used for purposes of sale or for the purposes of manufacture into butter, cheese, dried milk or condensed milk for sale, or in which vessels used for the sale of milk are kept, but

(ii) does not include a shop from which milk is supplied only in the properly closed and unopened vessels in which it is delivered to the shop, or a shop or other place in which milk is sold for consumption on the premises only;

(*b*) " dairy farm "—

(i) means any premises (being a dairy) on which milk is produced from cows, but

(ii) does not include any part of any such premises on which milk is manufactured into other products unless the milk produced on the premises

Meaning of " dairy ", " dairy farm " etc.

B

forms a substantial part of the milk so manufactured;

(c) "dairy farmer" means a dairyman who produces milk from cows; and

(d) "dairyman" includes an occupier of a dairy, a cow-keeper, and a purveyor of milk.

(2) If any question arises under paragraph (b)(ii) of subsection (1) whether the milk produced on a farm or other premises forms a substantial part of the milk that is manufactured into other products on that farm or on those premises, that question shall be determined by the Minister.

Milk and
Dairies
Regulations.

33.—(1) The Ministers may make regulations, called "Milk and Dairies Regulations", providing—

(a) for the inspection of cattle on dairy farms;

(b) for the inspection of dairies, and of persons in or about dairies who have access to the milk, or to the churns or other milk vessels;

(c) with respect to the lighting, ventilation, cleansing, drainage and water-supply of dairies;

(d) for securing the cleanliness of churns and other milk vessels and appliances and for prohibiting, subject to prescribed exceptions, the use of churns, (whether by the persons to whom they belong or other persons) otherwise than as containers for milk, where the churns are in use for the purposes of the business of a dairyman;

(e) for prescribing the precautions to be taken for protecting milk against infection or contamination;

(f) for preventing danger to health from the sale of infected, contaminated or dirty milk, and in particular for prohibiting the supply or sale of milk suspected of being infected;

(g) for imposing obligations on dairymen and their employees in regard to cases of infectious illness;

(h) for regulating the cooling, storage, conveyance and distribution of milk;

(j) with respect to the labelling, marking or identification, and the sealing or closing, of churns and other vessels used for the conveyance of milk, the labelling of vessels in which milk is sold or offered or exposed for sale or delivered, and the display of the vendor's name and address on any stall, or any cart, barrow or other vehicle; from which milk is sold or delivered;

(*k*) in cases where no express provision is made by this Act, for prohibiting or restricting—

    (i) the addition of any substance to milk, or the abstraction from milk of fat or any other constituent,

    (ii) the sale of milk to which any such addition, or from which any such abstraction, has been made, or which has been otherwise artificially treated ;

(*l*) for prohibiting or restricting, subject to prescribed exceptions, the sale for human consumption, as milk of any specified description, of milk containing less than a specified quantity of any specified normal constituent ;

(*m*) for requiring, subject to prescribed exceptions, cream or separated milk to be subjected to a specified treatment before being sold for human consumption ;

(*n*) for prohibiting, subject to prescribed exceptions, the sale for human consumption of milk obtained from cows milked—

    (i) at any stage of a journey to or from a dairy farm,

    (ii) at a slaughterhouse or knacker's yard, or

    (iii) in any market or other place where cattle are collected for the purposes of sale or showing, whether or not the market or place is registered in pursuance of Milk and Dairies Regulations as a dairy farm ;

(*o*) for requiring, subject to prescribed exceptions, any milk to which regulations in force under paragraph (*n*) apply to be stained or otherwise treated for the purposes of identification.

(2) In subsection (1)—

(*a*) " prescribed exceptions " means such exceptions as may be allowed by or under Milk and Dairies Regulations ; and

(*b*) except in paragraph (*o*), " milk " means milk intended for sale or sold for human consumption, or intended for manufacture into products for sale for human consumption.

(3) Paragraph (*m*) of subsection (1), so far as it relates to cream, shall be without prejudice to the power of the Ministers under section 4 to make regulations applying to cream, but regulations made under paragraph (*j*), paragraph (*k*) or paragraph (*l*) of that subsection shall not apply in relation to cream in so far

PART II as they are made for any purpose for which regulations relating to cream may be made under section 4.

(4) Milk and Dairies Regulations may be general regulations or regulations limited to a particular area.

Registration. 34.—(1) Milk and Dairies Regulations—

> (a) may provide for the registration of persons carrying on, or proposing to carry on, the trade of a dairyman and for the registration of dairies, and for prohibiting any person from carrying on that trade unless he and any premises used by him as a dairy are duly registered; and
>
> (b) shall provide for the registration by the Minister of dairy farms and of persons carrying on, or proposing to carry on, the trade of a dairy farmer.

(2) Regulations made for the purposes of this section may make special provision—

> (a) for the registration of premises used temporarily as dairies or dairy farms, and of the occupiers of such premises;
>
> (b) for the removal from the register of such premises and occupiers at the expiry of the period for which the registration is effected.

(3) Part I of Schedule 2 has effect, subject to subsection (5), with respect to refusing or cancelling the registration of dairymen.

(4) Subject to subsection (5), regulations made for the purposes of paragraph (b) of subsection (1) shall provide in accordance with Part II of Schedule 2 for dealing with the refusal and cancellation of any such registration as is mentioned in that paragraph.

(5) Schedule 2 does not apply to registration in pursuance of regulations made by virtue of subsection (2), or to persons registered or applying to be registered under them.

Sale of milk from diseased cows. 35.—(1) A person is guilty of an offence who—

> (a) sells, or offers or exposes for sale, for human consumption, or
>
> (b) uses in the manufacture of products for sale for human consumption,

the milk of any cow which to his knowledge has given tuberculous milk, or is suffering from emaciation due to tuberculosis, or from tuberculosis of the udder or any other disease of cows to which this section applies.

(2) In proceedings under this section, the defendant shall be deemed to have known that a cow had given tuberculous milk, or was suffering as mentioned above, if he could with ordinary care have ascertained the fact.

(3) The diseases of cows to which this section applies are those listed in Schedule 3 and any other disease to which the provisions of this section are extended by Milk and Dairies Regulations.

36.—(1) A person is guilty of an offence—   Adulteration.

    (a) who adds any water or colouring matter, or any dried or condensed milk or liquid reconstituted from it, to milk intended for sale for human consumption ;

    (b) who sells, or offers or exposes for sale, or has in his possession for the purpose of sale, for human consumption, any milk to which any addition has been made in contravention of paragraph (a) ;

    (c) who sells, or offers or exposes for sale, under the designation of milk, any liquid in the making of which any dried or condensed milk has been used.

(2) For the purposes of paragraph (b) of subsection (1), a person shall be deemed to retain the possession of milk which is deposited in any place for collection until it is actually collected.

(3) Nothing in subsection (2) shall be taken as prejudicing the defence available under section 81(4) to a person charged with an offence in respect of a sample of milk taken after the milk has left his possession.

(4) The treatment of milk by the application of steam shall not be treated for the purposes of this section as the making of an addition of water to that milk in contravention of the foregoing provisions of this section if—

    (a) Milk (Special Designation) Regulations under section 38 are in force prescribing a special designation in relation to milk subjected to that treatment ; and

    (b) that treatment is carried out in accordance with the conditions prescribed by those regulations as the conditions subject to which licences authorising the use of that special designation are granted ; and

    (c) those conditions include a condition that both the percentage of the milk consisting of milk fat and the percentage of the milk consisting of milk solids other than milk fat are the same after that treatment as before it.

37. The functions of veterinary inspectors under any enactments relating to milk or to dairies shall, in accordance with directions given by the Minister, be discharged by veterinary inspectors appointed for the purpose by him under section 5 of the Board of Agriculture Act 1889.

Special designations of milk, and their use

38.—(1) Provision may be made by regulations, to be made by the Ministers and called " Milk (Special Designation) Regulations "—

> (*a*) for prescribing, in relation to milk of any description, such designation (a " special designation ") as the Ministers consider appropriate ; and

> (*b*) for the granting of licences to producers and sellers of milk authorising the use of a special designation, and for prescribing the periods for which and the conditions subject to which licences, or licences of any particular class, are to be granted under the regulations.

(2) Provision made by such regulations for the granting of licences authorising the use of a special designation shall be for the granting of them by the following—

> (*a*) as respects licences authorising the use of a special designation of raw milk by the producer of the milk, the Minister ;

> (*b*) as respects other licences, either the Minister or county councils, food and drugs authorities or local authorities, as may be provided by the regulations.

(3) Part I of Schedule 4 has effect with respect to the provision by such regulations of—

> (*a*) the revocation or suspension of licences authorising the use of a special designation on the ground of a breach of condition of the licence ;

> (*b*) procedure in connection with decisions to revoke or suspend such licences or to refuse grants of such licences.

(4) The conditions prescribed by such regulations subject to which licences may be granted may include conditions as to the payment of fees.

39.—(1) A person is guilty of an offence who for the purpose of the sale or advertisement of any milk uses a special designation in any manner calculated to suggest that it refers to that milk, unless he holds a licence authorising the use of that designation in connection with that milk.

For the purpose of a sale or advertisement of milk as, or as part of, a meal or refreshments, a special designation may be used by a person who does not hold a licence authorising the use of that designation in connection with the milk if—

(a) the milk is milk bought by him; and

(b) that designation was used for the purpose of the sale of milk to him.

(2) A person is guilty of an offence who, for the purpose of the sale or advertisement of any milk, refers to that milk by any such description, not being a special designation, as is calculated falsely to suggest—

(a) that there is in force a licence authorising the use of a special designation in connection with that milk; or

(b) that the milk is tested, approved or graded by any competent person; or

(c) that the cows from which the milk is derived are free from the infection of tuberculosis or of any other disease.

(3) In any proceedings taken under subsection (2) it rests on the person charged to prove the truth of any suggestion which, in the court's opinion, his acts or conduct, as proved by the prosecution, are or is calculated to convey.

(4) Where there has been a breach of a condition subject to which a licence authorising the use of a special designation is granted, but the licence has not been revoked or suspended, the breach shall not be treated as rendering the use of the designation unauthorised for any of the purposes of this section or of any other provision of this Act.

(5) Section 47 applies for the interpretation of the references in this section to selling milk, but as if the definition of milk in that section were omitted.

*Compulsory use of special designations in specified areas,
and licences for specified areas*

40.—(1) The use of a special designation is obligatory for the purpose of all sales of milk by retail for human consumption (other than catering sales) where the place of sale is in an area in which this subsection is in operation under the following provisions of this Part in that behalf, and subject to this Part.

(2) An area in which subsection (1) is in operation as there mentioned is in this Part, and in Schedule 4, referred to as " a specified area ".

(3) Notwithstanding that the place of sale is not in a specified area, the use of a special designation is obligatory also for the purpose of a sale of milk by retail for human consumption (other than a catering sale) if—

> (a) the milk is delivered from an establishment, whether in or outside a specified area ; and

> (b) there is carried on at that establishment a business of selling milk which includes any sales for the purpose of which the use of a special designation is obligatory under subsection (1).

(4) Subsections (1) and (3) do not apply to the selling of milk as mentioned in those subsections by a producer of milk from cows to persons—

> (a) employed by him in or in connection with such production, or

> (b) employed by him otherwise in agriculture,

if he does not engage in any other selling of milk as mentioned in those subsections.

(5) A person who sells milk without the use of a special designation under a sale for the purpose of which the use of a special designation is obligatory by virtue of this section is guilty of an offence.

(6) Section 47 applies for the interpretation of this section.

Special
designations:
catering.

41.—(1) This section applies—

> (a) to catering sales ; and

> (b) to sales of milk to a person who carries on a business which consists of or comprises making catering sales (in this section called " a caterer ").

(2) Subject to this Part, a catering sale made in a specified area—

> (a) is lawful (unless it is for any reason unlawful apart from this subsection) if the caterer bought the milk under a sale for the purpose of which a special designation was used, or if he holds a licence authorising him to use a special designation in connection with the milk, whether the designation is used for the purpose of the catering sale or not, but

> (b) otherwise shall be unlawful.

(3) Subject to this Part, on a sale of milk to a caterer, being a sale for the purpose of which the use of a special designation would be obligatory by section 40 if it were a sale by retail, the use of such a designation is obligatory, except where—

(a) the caterer buys the milk with a view to subjecting it to a process to which milk is required to be subjected as a condition of the use of a special designation in connection with it, and he is the holder of a licence authorising him to use that designation ; or

(b) the caterer buys the milk for the purposes of a business of his as a milk dealer or a manufacturer of milk products other than his business as a caterer.

(4) A person is guilty of an offence—

(a) who makes a catering sale which is unlawful under subsection (2) ; or

(b) who sells milk without the use of a special designation under a sale for the purpose of which the use of a special designation is obligatory under subsection (3).

(5) A person is not guilty of an offence under subsection (3) if at the time of the sale in question he had reasonable cause to believe that the conditions specified in paragraph (a) or paragraph (b) of that subsection were satisfied as to that sale or that the buyer was not a caterer.

(6) Section 47 applies for the interpretation of this section.

42.—(1) Notwithstanding anything in subsection (1) or subsection (3) of section 40, or in section 41(3), selling milk as mentioned in those subsections without the use of a special designation is permissible if done with the Minister's consent.

Special designations: exemption.

(2) The Minister may give consents for the purposes of this section—

(a) either generally as respects selling milk as mentioned in those subsections or restricted to a particular retailer or establishment or otherwise, and

(b) either unconditionally or subject to conditions,

as may appear to him to be requisite to meet any circumstances in which use of a special designation which would be obligatory under those subsections apart from the consent appears to him to be for the time being not reasonably practicable.

(3) A catering sale made in a specified area is not unlawful under section 41(2) if the milk was sold to the caterer with consent given by the Minister for the purposes of this section.

(4) Section 47 applies for the interpretation of this section.

Specified
areas.

43.—(1) The Ministers may at any time order that section 40(1) shall come into operation in any area in which it is not then in operation, or shall cease to be in operation in any area in which it is then in operation.

(2) Before making an order under this section the Ministers shall consult with such representative organisations as appear to them substantially to represent the interests concerned with the purposes of the order.

(3) For the purposes of this Part—

    (*a*) if a contract of sale of milk is made in one place and the milk is delivered under the contract in another place, the place of sale shall, except in a case falling within paragraph (*b*), be taken to be the place where the milk is so delivered ;

    (*b*) if a contract of sale of milk is made in one place and the milk is delivered under the contract to a carrier for transport to another place, the place of the sale shall be taken to be that other place.

(4) Part II of Schedule 4 has effect as respects the application of Part I of that Schedule to a licence held by a retailer for a specified area.

(5) Section 47 applies for the interpretation of this section.

Milk
processing
facilities.

44.—(1) The Minister may—

    (*a*) install, maintain and operate apparatus for the subjection of milk to any process to which it is required to be subjected as a condition of the use of a special designation in connection with it, and

    (*b*) provide any other facilities for that purpose,

in any case in which it appears to him as respects—

    (i) any area which is a specified area, or

    (ii) an area as to which the Ministers propose to make an order bringing section 40(1) into operation,

that facilities for the application of such treatment sufficient to provide for supplies of milk of that designation in that area in requisite quantities are not available and are not likely otherwise to become available.

(2) Where the Minister provides facilities under this section—

   (*a*) he may either buy the milk to be treated and re-sell it, otherwise than by retail or to a caterer for the purposes of his business as such, after treatment ; or

   (*b*) apply the treatment to milk of others.

(3) The Minister may arrange with local authorities or other persons for the doing, on his behalf and at his expense, of things which he is authorised by this section to do, and it shall be within the powers of local authorities to carry out arrangements so made.

(4) Section 47 applies for the interpretation of this section ; and in this section " local authority " means a local authority within the meaning of the Local Government Act 1972.   1972 c. 70.

45.—(1) In the event of a breach of any condition to which this section applies of a licence held by a retailer for a specified area, the holder of the licence shall be guilty of an offence under this section, subject to section 46.   Breach of retailer's licence.

(2) The conditions to which this section applies are conditions as to any such matters as are specified in Schedule 5.

(3) Milk (Special Designation) Regulations shall specify the authorities, whether local authorities or food and drugs authorities, by whom the provisions of this section are to be enforced as respects licences other than licences which authorise the use—

   (*a*) of a special designation in relation to raw milk by its producer ; or

   (*b*) of a special designation by a local authority.

(4) Section 47 applies for the interpretation of this section ; and in this section " local authority " means a local authority within the meaning of the Local Government Act 1972.

46.—(1) Such a breach of condition as is mentioned in section 45, constituted by an act or omission for which the holder of the licence is liable to any punishment imposed by or under any enactment other than that section, does not render the holder of the licence guilty of an offence under that section.   Restriction on liability under s. 45.

(2) Such a breach of condition as is mentioned in section 45 does not render the holder of the licence guilty of an offence under that section unless it was the later, or a later, of two or more such breaches, occurring within a period of 12 months, of conditions either of that licence or of that licence and a

PART II   former licence by way of renewal of which that licence was granted, and was committed either—

(a) after the licensing authority had given him notice in writing as to an earlier of those two or more breaches informing him of his being alleged to have committed it, and warning him of the liability to prosecution imposed by section 45 ; or

(b) after he had been convicted of an offence under that section because of an earlier of those two or more breaches.

(3) In the case of any prosecution in respect of such a breach of condition as is mentioned in section 45 which would otherwise render the holder of the licence guilty of an offence under that section, it is a defence for him to prove the following matters (either as to that breach, or as to the earlier breach relied on for the purpose of subsection (2) of this section, unless it is one under which he has been convicted of such an offence)—

(a) that neither he nor any servant or agent of his—

(i) did or knew of the doing of, any act that constituted the breach or can reasonably be regarded as having been the cause or among the causes of it, or

(ii) omitted to do, or knew of an omission to do, any act the omission of which constituted the breach, or the doing of which can reasonably be regarded as a precaution that would have prevented it ; and

(b) if the breach was in connection with milk that had been sold to him, or had been delivered to him after being subjected to a process to which it was required to be subjected as a condition of the use of the special designation to which his licence related, that that designation—

(i) was used for the purpose of the sale to him or in connection with the delivery to him, as the case may be, and

(ii) was so used without any breach, discoverable by the exercise of reasonable diligence on the part of himself or any servant or agent of his, of any condition, relating to receptacles, to closing, to fastening or to marking, of a licence to use that designation held by the person who sold the milk to him or subjected it to the process, as the case may be.

(4) Section 47 applies for the interpretation of this section.

47. In sections 39, 40, 41, 42, 43, 44, 45 and 46, in this section, and in Schedules 4 and 5, except where the context otherwise requires—

" business " includes the business of a hospital, school or other institution the selling of milk by which is incidental only to the rendering of the health, education or other services rendered by the institution ;

" catering sale " means a sale of milk, or of things made from milk or of which milk is an ingredient, as, or as part of, a meal or refreshments ;

" licence held by a retailer for a specified area " means a licence authorising the use of a special designation held by a person carrying on a business which includes any sales which are sales for the purpose of which the use of a special designation is obligatory by virtue of this Part and are of milk in relation to which that licence authorises the use of a special designation ;

" licensing authority " means, in relation to a grant of a licence authorising the use of a special designation, the authority having power to grant the licence by virtue of Milk (Special Designation) Regulations, and, in relation to such a licence which has been granted, the authority who would for the time being have power by virtue of such regulations as mentioned above to grant a licence by way of its renewal if it had expired ;

" milk " means cows' milk, excluding not only condensed milk and dried milk, but also cream and separated, skimmed and evaporated milk, and butter milk ;

" selling " means selling in the course of a business and includes, in relation to milk, supplying it under arrangements for free supply, and, in relation to milk and things made from milk or of which milk is an ingredient, supplying it or them, in the course of any business otherwise than under such arrangements ; and references to sales and contracts of sale and sellers shall be construed accordingly ;

" selling milk by retail " means selling it—

    (a) to any person other than a milk dealer (that is, a person who carries on a business which consists of or comprises the selling of milk) or a manufacturer of milk products (that is, a person who carries on a business which consists of or comprises the making of things made from milk or of which milk is an ingredient), or

    (b) to such a dealer or manufacturer otherwise than for the purposes of his business as such ;

" specified area " has the meaning given by section 40(2) ;

" supplying under arrangements for free supply " means, in relation to any milk, supplying it, free from any payments made or to be made by the person to whom it is supplied, under arrangements made in exercise of powers in that behalf conferred by section 78(2) of the Education Act 1944, or section 22 of the Education Act 1980, or any regulation under the Emergency Laws (Re-enactments and Repeals) Act 1964 ; and references to a person's buying milk include references to his having it supplied to him under such arrangements.

1944 c. 31.
1980 c. 20.
1964 c. 60.

Cream substitutes

Misuse of designation " cream ".

48.—(1) A person is guilty of an offence who sells, or offers or exposes for sale, for human consumption—

(*a*) any substance which resembles cream in appearance, but is not cream, or

(*b*) any article of food containing such a substance,

under a description or designation which includes the word " cream " (whether or not as part of a composite word).

(2) Subsection (1) does not apply to the sale, or offer or exposure for sale—

(*a*) of any substance being reconstituted or imitation cream as defined by this section, or of any article containing such a substance, under a description or designation which identifies the substance as such ; or

(*b*) of any substance under a description or designation which indicates that the substance is not for use as, or as a substitute for, cream.

(3) In this section " reconstituted cream " means a substance which, not being cream, resembles cream in appearance and contains no ingredient not derived from milk, except—

(*a*) water, or

(*b*) ingredients (not added fraudulently to increase bulk, weight or measure, or conceal inferior quality) which may lawfully be contained in a substance sold for human consumption as cream,

and " imitation cream " means a substance which, not being cream or reconstituted cream, resembles cream in appearance and is produced by emulsifying edible oils or fats with water, either by themselves or with other substances which are neither prohibited by regulations made for the purposes of this section under section 4, nor added in quantities so prohibited.

(4) For the purposes of this section, the description or designation under which a substance or article is sold, or offered

or exposed for sale, shall be deemed to include the word "cream" if it includes any other word (composite or otherwise) which is calculated to lead a purchaser to suppose that the substance is or, as the case may be, the article contains either cream or a substance for use as cream.

49. Such of the following provisions as apply in relation to cream—

Reconstituted cream.

(a) any provision of this Part,

(b) any provisions of Milk and Dairies Regulations, other than provisions relating to the registration of dairymen and dairies, and

(c) any provision of Milk (Special Designation) Regulations,

also apply in relation to reconstituted cream as defined by section 48, save as otherwise expressly provided.

PART III

MARKETS

50.—(1) The council of a district may—

Establishment or acquisition.

(a) establish a market within their district ;

(b) acquire by agreement (but not otherwise), either by purchase or on lease, the whole or any part of an existing market undertaking within their district, and any rights enjoyed by any person within their district in respect of a market and of tolls,

and, in either case, may provide—

(i) a market place with convenient approaches to it ;

(ii) a market house and other buildings convenient for the holding of a market.

(2) A market shall not be established in pursuance of this section so as to interfere with any rights, powers or privileges enjoyed within the district in respect of a market by any person, without that person's consent.

(3) For the purposes of subsection (2), another local authority shall not be deemed to be enjoying any rights, powers or privileges within the district by reason only of the fact that they have established a market within their own district either—

(a) under paragraph (a) of subsection (1) ; or

(b) under the corresponding provision of either the Food and Drugs Act 1955 or the Food and Drugs Act 1938 ; or

1955 c. 16.
(4 & 5 Eliz. 2)
1938 c. 56.

PART III
1875 c. 55.

(c) under any corresponding provision repealed by that Act of 1938 or the Public Health Act 1875, otherwise than by acquisition of a then existing market.

Power to sell to local authority.

51.—(1) The owner of a market undertaking, or of any rights in respect of a market and of tolls, whether established under, or enjoyed by virtue of, statutory powers or not, may sell or lease to a local authority the whole or any part of his market undertaking or rights, but subject to all attached liabilities.

(2) A sale by a market company under this section must be authorised—

1948 c. 38.

(a) if the company is a company within the meaning of the Companies Act 1948, by a special resolution of the members passed in the manner provided in Part IV of that Act;

(b) if the company is not such a company, by a resolution passed by three-fourths in number and value of the members present, either personally or by proxy, at a meeting specially convened for the purpose with notice of the business to be transacted.

Market days and hours.

52. A market authority may appoint the days on which, and the hours during which, markets are to be held.

Charges.

53.—(1) A market authority may demand in respect of the market, and in respect of the weighing and measuring of articles and vehicles, such charges as they may from time to time determine.

(2) A market authority who provide a weighing machine for weighing cattle, sheep or swine may demand in respect of the weighing of such animals such charges as the authority may from time to time determine.

(3) The authority—

(a) shall keep exhibited in conspicuous places in the market place, and in any market house, tables stating in large and legibly printed characters the several charges payable under this Part; and

(b) shall keep so much of the tables as relates to charges payable in respect of the weighing of vehicles, or, as the case may be, in respect of the weighing of animals, conspicuously exhibited at every weighing machine provided by them in connection with the market for the purpose.

(4) A person who demands or accepts a charge greater than that for the time being authorised shall be liable to a fine not exceeding level 2 on the standard scale.

(5) Nothing in this section applies in relation to rents charged by a market authority in respect of the letting of accommodation within their market for any period longer than one week.

54.—(1) Charges payable in respect of the market shall be paid from time to time on demand to an authorised market officer.

(2) Charges payable in respect of the weighing or measuring of articles, vehicles or animals shall be paid in advance to an authorised market officer by the persons bringing the articles, vehicles or animals to be weighed or measured.

(3) Charges payable in respect of animals brought to the market for sale shall be payable, and may be demanded by an authorised market officer—

(*a*) as soon as the animals in respect of which they are payable are brought into the market place, and

(*b*) before they are put into any pen, or tied up in the market place,

but further charges shall be payable and may be demanded in respect of any of the animals which are not removed within one hour after the close of the market.

55. If a person liable to pay any charge authorised under this Part does not pay it when lawfully demanded, the market authority may, by any authorised market officer, levy it by distress—

(*a*) of all or any of the animals, poultry or other articles in respect of which the charge is payable, or

(*b*) of any other animals, poultry or articles in the market belonging to, or in the charge of, the person liable,

and any such charge may also be recovered either summarily as a civil debt or in any court of competent jurisdiction.

56.—(1) A person (other than a pedlar holding a certificate under the Pedlars Act 1871) who on a market day and during market hours sells or exposes for sale any articles—

(*a*) which are specified in a byelaw made by the market authority, and

(*b*) which are commonly sold in the market,

and such sale or exposure for sale—

(i) is in any place within the authority's district, and

(ii) is within such distance from the market as the authority may by byelaw declare,

is liable to a fine not exceeding level 2 on the standard scale.

This subsection does not apply to a sale or exposure for sale in a person's own dwelling place or shop, or in, or at the door of, any premises to a person resident in those premises.

(2) The market authority shall keep exhibited in conspicuous positions in the vicinity of the market notices stating the effect of any byelaw made under this section.

Weighing machines and scales.

57.—(1) A market authority—

(a) shall provide sufficient scales, weights, measures and weighing machines for weighing or measuring articles sold in the market and vehicles in which articles are brought for sale in the market ; and

(b) shall appoint officers to attend to the weighing and measuring of such articles and vehicles.

(2) A market authority in whose market cattle, sheep or swine are sold shall, unless there is in force an order of the Minister declaring that the circumstances are such as to render compliance with this subsection unnecessary—

(a) provide to that Minister's satisfaction one or more weighing machines adapted for weighing such animals ; and

(b) appoint officers to attend to the weighing of such animals.

1926 c. 21.

A weighing machine provided under this subsection shall for the purposes of section 1 of the Markets and Fairs (Weighing of Cattle) Act 1926, be deemed to have been provided for the purpose of complying with the provisions of the principal Act referred to in that Act of 1926.

Weighing of articles.

58. A person who sells or offers for sale any articles in the market shall, if so required by the buyer, cause them to be weighed or measured by the scales and weights or measures provided by the market authority, and, if he refuses to do so, shall be liable to a fine not exceeding level 2 on the standard scale.

Information for market officer.

59. The person in charge of any vehicle in which, and any other person by whom, animals, poultry or other articles are brought for sale in the market shall give to any authorised market officer such information—

(a) as to their number and kind, or

(b) in the case of articles on which charges are made by reference to weight, as to their weight,

as that officer may require.

60. A local authority who maintain a market, whether or not they are a market authority within the meaning of this Act, may make byelaws— PART III
Market
byelaws.

    (a) for regulating the use of the market place, and the buildings, stalls, pens and standings in that market place ;

    (b) for preventing nuisances or obstructions in the market place, or in the immediate approaches to it ;

    (c) for regulating porters and carriers resorting to the market, and fixing the charges to be made for carrying articles from the market within the district.

61. In this Part, unless the context otherwise requires— Interpretation of Part III, and exclusion of City of London.

    " authorised market officer " means an officer of a market authority specially authorised by them to collect charges in their market,

    " charges " includes stallage or tolls,

    " market authority " means a local authority who have established or acquired a market under section 50 of this Act, or under section 49 of the Food and Drugs Act 1955, or under the corresponding enactment repealed by that Act, and so on, and includes any London borough council to whom a market was transferred by the London Authorities (Property etc.) Order 1964, 1955 c. 16 (4 & 5 Eliz 2).

S.I. 1964/1464.

and this Part does not apply to the City of London, the Inner Temple or the Middle Temple.

PART IV

SALE OF FOOD BY HAWKERS

62. A local authority may resolve that this Part is to apply to their area, and if a local authority do so resolve— Application of Part IV.

    (a) this Part shall come into force in their area on the day specified in that behalf in the resolution ; but

    (b) that day must not be before the expiry of the period of one month beginning with the day on which the resolution is passed.

63. Where a local authority have passed a resolution under this Part, they shall publish a notice for two consecutive weeks, in a local newspaper circulating in their area, which shall state— Public notice of application of Part IV.

    (a) that the resolution has been passed, and

    (b) the general effect of the following provisions of this Part.

and the first publication of that notice shall not be later than 28 days before the day specified in the resolution for the coming into force of this Part in the local authority's area.

Registration of food hawkers, and their premises.

64.—(1) In any area in which this and the following sections of this Part are in force—

   (*a*) no person shall hawk food unless he is registered under those sections by the local authority for the area ; and

   (*b*) no premises shall be used as storage accommodation for any food intended for hawking unless the premises are so registered.

This subsection applies to a person who hawks food as an assistant to a person registered under those sections unless—

   (i) he is normally supervised when so doing ; or

   (ii) he assists only as a temporary replacement.

(2) For the purposes of those sections a person hawks food if for private gain—

   (*a*) he goes from place to place selling food or offering or exposing food for sale, or

   (*b*) he sells food in the open air or offers or exposes food for sale in the open air,

unless he does so as part of, or as an activity ancillary to, a trade or business carried on by him or some other person on identifiable property.

Contravention of s. 64, and defence.

65.—(1) A person who without reasonable excuse contravenes section 64 is guilty of an offence and liable on summary conviction to a fine not exceeding level 3 on the standard scale.

(2) It is a defence for a person charged with such an offence to prove that he—

   (*a*) took all reasonable precautions, and

   (*b*) exercised all due diligence,

to avoid committing the offence.

Application for registration.

66.—(1) An application for registration under this Part shall be accompanied by such particulars as the local authority may reasonably require.

(2) The particulars that the local authority may require include, without prejudice to the generality of subsection (1), particulars as to any vehicle to be used by the applicant in connection with food hawking.

(3) A local authority may charge such reasonable fees as they may determine for registration under this Part.

(4) An application for premises to be registered under this Part shall be made by the person intending to use them as storage accommodation.

(5) On application for registration under this Part the local authority shall—

    (*a*) register the applicant and, if the application is for the registration of premises, those premises ; and

    (*b*) issue to the applicant a certificate of registration.

67.—(1) In this Part, " food " means food and ingredients of food for human consumption, including—

    (*a*) drink (other than water) ;

    (*b*) chewing gum and like products ;

but does not include—

    (i) milk and cream ;

    (ii) live animals or birds ;

    (iii) articles or substances used only as drugs.

(2) Parts VI and VII do not apply for the purposes of this Part, except for—

    (*a*) the definition of " local authority " in section 72 ;

    (*b*) the definition of " standard scale " in section 132(1) ; and

    (*c*) section 134, and paragraph 1 of Schedule 9, Schedule 11, and section 136.

(3) This Part does not apply—

    (*a*) to the sale or offer or exposure for sale of food—

        (i) at a market or fair the right to hold which was acquired by virtue of a grant (including a presumed grant) or acquired or established by virtue of an enactment or order ;

        (ii) at a notified temporary market ; or

        (iii) at a notified pleasure fair ; or

    (*b*) to the sale or offer or exposure for sale of food in or from premises exempt from registration by paragraphs (*c*) and (*d*) of section 16(3) or of food prepared or manufactured on such premises ; or

    (*c*) to the sale or offer or exposure for sale of food by way of street trading at any place in the local authority's area by a person whom the local authority have authorised under any enactment to engage in such trading in their area (whether or not they have authorised him to trade at the place where the food was sold or offered or exposed for sale) or by a person acting as an assistant to a person so authorised ; or

PART IV

(d) to premises used as storage accommodation for food prepared for sale as mentioned in paragraphs (a) to (c) above; or

(e) to the sale or offer or exposure for sale of food in containers of such materials and so closed as to exclude all risks of contamination.

In this subsection—

"notified pleasure fair" means a pleasure fair, as defined in paragraph (a) of section 75(2) of the Public Health Act 1961, notice of which has been given to the local authority in accordance with byelaws under that section;

1961 c. 64.

"notified temporary market" means a temporary market notice of which has been given to the local authority in accordance with section 37(2) of the Local Government (Miscellaneous Provisions) Act 1982 or any other enactment regulating such markets.

1982 c. 30.

PART V

SUGAR BEET AND COLD STORAGE

Ministerial functions as to sugar beet

Research and education.

68.—(1) The appropriate Minister, after consultation with the Company and with any body which in that Minister's opinion is substantially representative of growers of home-grown beet—

(a) shall prepare for each year a programme for carrying out research and education in matters affecting the growing of home-grown beet; and

(b) may by order provide for carrying any such programme into effect.

(2) Any such programme for any year shall contain an estimate of the amount of the expenditure to be incurred in carrying it out; and any order made for carrying such a programme into effect shall, in particular, provide—

(a) for assessing the contributions towards defraying such expenditure to be made by the Company and by every grower of home-grown beet who delivers beet to the Company in that year; and

(b) for the collection of such contributions and the recovery of unpaid contributions by the appropriate Minister.

(3) All contributions paid in accordance with an order under subsection (1) shall be paid into a research and education fund.

(4) All expenditure certified by the appropriate Minister to have been properly incurred in carrying out any programme prepared under this section (including expenditure incurred by him or on his behalf) shall be defrayed out of the fund mentioned in subsection (3).

(5) That fund shall be under the Minister's control; and an account showing the revenue and expenditure of the fund for any year shall, not later than 30th November in the year following that to which it relates, be transmitted by the Minister to the Comptroller and Auditor General, who shall examine and certify the account and lay copies of it, together with his report on it, before Parliament.

(6) In this section—

" the appropriate Minister "—

> (a) in relation to a programme or order extending to the whole of Great Britain, means the Minister of Agriculture, Fisheries and Food, the Secretary of State for Scotland and the Secretary of State for Wales, acting jointly,

> (b) in relation to a programme or order extending only to England and Wales, means the Minister and the Secretary of State, acting jointly,

> (c) in relation to a programme or order extending only to Scotland, means the Secretary of State ;

" the Company " means British Sugar, public limited company ;

" financial year of the Company " means the 12 months beginning with 1st April ;

" home-grown beet " means sugar beet grown in Great Britain ;

" year " means a financial year of the Company.

69.—(1) If as regards the home-grown beet crop for any year Crop price. it is made to appear to the Ministers—

(a) by the processors of home-grown beet, or

(b) by a body which is in their opinion substantially representative of the growers of home-grown beet,

that the processors and that body are unable to agree on the prices and other terms and conditions for the purchase of home-grown beet by the processors, the Ministers may determine or designate a person to determine those prices, terms and conditions.

(2) Any purchase by processors for which prices, terms and conditions have been so determined, or contract for such a purchase, shall take effect as a purchase or contract for purchase at those prices and on those terms and conditions.

PART V

(3) In this section "home-grown beet" means sugar beet grown in Great Britain; and "the Ministers" means the Minister of Agriculture, Fisheries and Food, the Secretary of State for Scotland and the Secretary of State for Wales, acting jointly.

Cold storage

Provision of cold storage.

70.—(1) A local authority who have provided or are about to provide a market may—

    (a) provide a cold air store or refrigerator for the storage and preservation of meat and other articles of food; and

    (b) make charges in respect of the use of any such store or refrigerator.

(2) Any proposal by a local authority to provide under this section a cold air store or refrigerator within the district of another local authority requires the consent of that other authority.

(3) Such consent shall not be unreasonably withheld and any question whether or not the consent of an authority for the purposes of subsection (2) is unreasonably withheld shall be referred to and determined by the Minister.

1972 c. 70.

(4) Subsections (1) to (5) of section 250 of the Local Government Act 1972 (which relate to local inquiries) shall apply for the purposes of this section as if any reference in those subsections to that Act included a reference to this section.

PART VI

ADMINISTRATION, ENFORCEMENT AND LEGAL PROCEEDINGS

Administration

Food and drugs authorities.

71. The food and drugs authority shall continue to be—

    (a) in England, for each county and London borough, the council of that county or borough, and for the City of London and the Inner Temple and the Middle Temple, the Common Council of the City of London;

    (b) in Wales, the county council.

Local authorities for purposes of this Act.

72. In this Act, except in sections 44 and 45, "local authority" means—

    (a) as respects the City of London, the Common Council;

    (b) as respects the Inner Temple and the Middle Temple, the Sub-Treasurer and the Under Treasurer respectively; and

    (c) as respects any district or London borough, the council of the district or borough.

73.—(1) "Authorised officer", where used in this Act in
relation to a council—

> (a) means an officer of the council authorised by them in
> writing, either generally or specially, to act in matters
> of any specified kind or in any specified matter ; and
>
> (b) for the purposes of any provision of this Act relating to
> the taking of samples, includes a police constable so
> authorised with the approval of the police authority
> concerned.

(2) No officer of a council shall be authorised under this
Act to act in relation to the examination and seizure of meat
unless he is a person having such qualifications as may be prescribed by regulations made by the Ministers.

74.—(1) The Minister shall enforce and execute the provisions
of the sections, orders and regulations specified in paragraph 1
of Schedule 6, and the food and drugs authorities shall enforce
and execute the provisions of the sections and regulations specified in paragraph 2 of that Schedule.

(2) It is the duty of every local authority to enforce and
execute in their district the provisions of any section of this
Act with respect to which the duty is not expressly, or by necessary implication, imposed on some other authority.

(3) Regulations made under Part I, Milk and Dairies Regulations and Milk (Special Designation) Regulations shall specify
the authorities by whom they are to be enforced and executed,
being—

> (a) in the case of regulations made under Part I, county
> councils, local authorities, food and drugs authorities,
> port health authorities, or the Commissioners of Cus-
> toms and Excise,
>
> (b) in the case of Milk and Dairies Regulations and Milk
> (Special Designation) Regulations, county councils,
> local authorities, food and drugs authorities, or port
> health authorities,

and any regulations to which this subsection applies may provide
for the giving of assistance and information, by any authority
concerned in the administration of the regulations, or of this
Act, to any other authority so concerned, for the purposes of
their respective duties under them.

This subsection does not apply to the enforcement and execution of so much of any regulations made under Part II as is,
by virtue of subsection (1), enforceable by the Minister.

PART VI

(4) Subsection (3) applies to Northern Ireland so far as it relates—

   (a) to those regulations and orders made under Part I which apply to Northern Ireland ; and

   (b) to the enforcement and execution of those regulations and orders,

and accordingly that subsection is modified—

   (i) by the substitution in paragraph (a) of the words " district councils " for " county councils, local authorities, food and drugs authorities, port health authorities " ; and

   (ii) by the construction of the reference to any authority concerned in the administration of this Act as a reference to any authority concerned in the administration of any corresponding Northern Ireland enactment.

Joint boards.
1936 c. 49.

75. An order made by the Secretary of State under section 6 of the Public Health Act 1936 may constitute a united district for the purposes of any functions under this Act which are functions of a local authority, whether as a food and drugs authority or otherwise.

Sampling and analysis

Public
analysts.

76.—(1) Every food and drugs authority shall appoint in accordance with this section one or more persons (in this Act called " public analysts ") to be analysts of food and drugs within their area.

(2) No person shall be appointed a public analyst unless he possesses either—

   (a) the qualifications prescribed by regulations made by the Ministers, or

   (b) such other qualifications as the Ministers may approve,

and no person shall be appointed public analyst for any area who is engaged directly or indirectly in any trade or business connected with the sale of food or drugs in that area.

(3) A food and drugs authority shall pay to a public analyst such remuneration as may be agreed, which may be expressed to be payable either—

   (a) in addition to any fees received by him under this Part ; or

   (b) on condition that any fees so received by him are paid over by him to the authority.

(4) A food and drugs authority who appoint only one public analyst may appoint also a deputy to act during any vacancy

in the office of public analyst, or during the absence or incapacity of the holder of the office, and— PART VI

(a) the provisions of this section with respect to the qualifications, appointment, removal and remuneration of a public analyst shall apply also in relation to a deputy public analyst; and

(b) any reference in the following provisions of this Act to a public analyst shall be construed as including a reference to a deputy public analyst appointed under this subsection.

77. A county council or local authority may provide facilities for bacteriological and other examinations of samples of food and drugs. Facilities for examination.

78.—(1) An authorised officer of a council may exercise such powers of procuring samples for analysis, or for bacteriological or other examination, as are conferred upon him by this section, and any such officer is in this Act called a "sampling officer". Powers of sampling.

(2) A sampling officer may purchase samples of any food or of any substance capable of being used in the preparation of food.

(3) A sampling officer may take a sample of any food, or of any substance capable of being used in the preparation of food, which—

(a) appears to him to be intended for sale, or to have been sold, for human consumption; or

(b) is found by him on or in any premises, stall, vehicle, ship, aircraft or place which he is authorised to enter for the purposes of the execution of this Act.

(4) Without prejudice to subsection (3), a sampling officer—

(a) may take a sample of milk while at any dairy, or while deposited for collection, or at any time before it is delivered to a consumer in pursuance of a sale by retail;

(b) may, at the request of a person to whom any food or substance is, or is to be, delivered in pursuance of a contract of sale, take a sample of that food or substance in the course of delivery, or at the place of delivery.

(5) A sampling officer who under this section takes a sample of the milk of any cows at a dairy may take such steps at the dairy as may be necessary to satisfy himself that the sample is a fair sample of the milk of the cows when properly and fully milked.

(6) Except as provided by subsection (4), or with the purchaser's consent, a sampling officer shall not take a sample of

any food or substance which appears to him to have been sold by retail, either—

> (*a*) while the food or substance is in the course of delivery to the purchaser, or
>
> (*b*) at any time after such delivery,

and nothing in this section shall authorise a sampling officer to take a sample of any food or substance in a ship (not being a home-going ship) or in any aircraft, other than food imported as part of the cargo of that ship or aircraft.

(7) The powers of taking samples of milk which are conferred on a sampling officer by subsections (3) to (6) shall be exercisable throughout any county by an authorised officer of the county council, whether or not the council is the food and drugs authority for the whole county.

(8) Any power of an authorised officer in respect of procuring samples of milk may be exercised at a place outside the area of the council whose officer he is, if the food and drugs authority of the area within which that place is situated have consented to samples of milk being procured within their areas by officers of the first-mentioned council, and, for the purposes of this Act, any samples so procured shall be deemed to have been procured within the area for which the officer in question acts.

A food and drugs authority shall not unreasonably withhold their consent for the purposes of this subsection ; and any question whether or not such consent is unreasonably withheld shall be referred to and determined by the Secretary of State.

Right to have samples analysed.

79.—(1) If a sampling officer who has procured a sample of any food or substance considers that it should be analysed, he shall submit it to be analysed by the public analyst for the area in which the sample was, or is deemed to have been, procured.

(2) A person, other than a sampling officer, who has purchased any food, or any substance capable of being used in the preparation of food, may submit a sample of it to be analysed by the public analyst for the area in which the purchase was made.

(3) The public analyst shall analyse as soon as practicable any sample submitted to him in pursuance of this section, but may, in the case of a sample submitted by a person not being an officer of the food and drugs authority, demand in advance the payment of such fee as may be fixed by the authority.

(4) If—

> (*a*) the office of public analyst for the area in question is vacant, or
>
> (*b*) the public analyst determines that he is for any reason unable to perform an effective analysis,

the sample shall be submitted or, as the case may be, sent by the public analyst to whom it was originally submitted, to the public analyst for some other area, and he shall, upon payment to him of such sum as may be agreed, analyse the sample.

(5) A public analyst who has analysed a sample shall give to the person by whom it was originally submitted a certificate specifying the result of the analysis ; and any such certificate shall be in a form prescribed by regulations made by the Ministers.

(6) Any certificate of the results of an analysis given by a public analyst in pursuance of this section shall be signed by the public analyst, but the analysis may be made by any person acting under the direction of the analyst.

80.—(1) A sampling officer who purchases or takes a sample of any food or substance for the purpose of analysis by a public analyst shall deal with the sample in accordance with Part I of Schedule 7.

(2) Part I of that Schedule applies to the purchase of samples by any person who is neither a sampling officer nor a person having the powers of a sampling officer as it applies in relation to the purchase of samples by a sampling officer ; and references in that Part to a sampling officer shall be construed accordingly.

(3) If it appears to a sampling officer that any food or substance, of which he has procured a sample for the purpose of analysis by a public analyst, was manufactured or put into its wrapper or container by a person (not being a person to whom one part of the sample is required to be given under Part I of Schedule 7) having his name and an address in the United Kingdom displayed on the wrapper or container, the officer shall, unless he decides not to have an analysis made, within three days of procuring the sample send to that person a notice informing him—

(a) that the sample has been procured by the officer ; and

(b) where the sample was taken or, as the case may be, from whom it was purchased.

(4) Where a sample taken or purchased by a sampling officer has been analysed by a public analyst, any person to whom a part of the sample was given under Part I of Schedule 7 shall be entitled, on payment to the authority by whose officer the sample was procured of a fee of 5p to be supplied with a copy of the certificate given by the public analyst under section 79(5).

81.—(1) The provisions of this Act relating—

(a) to the procuring of samples by a sampling officer, and

Samples taken for analysis.

Sampling of milk.

(*b*) to connected proceedings,

have in relation to milk effect subject to Part II of Schedule 7.

(2) Where milk sold or exposed for sale within the area of any council is obtained from a dairy outside that area—

    (*a*) the proper officer or any other authorised officer of the council may by written notice to the proper officer or other authorised officer of a food and drugs authority within whose area the dairy is situated, or through whose area the milk is transported, request him to procure samples of the milk, and

    (*b*) it is the duty of an officer who receives such a notice to procure, as soon as is practicable, samples of the milk in question and to forward those samples to the officer who gave the notice, or to such person as that officer may direct,

and for the purposes of this Act samples so procured shall be deemed to have been procured within the area for which the officer who gave the notice acts.

(3) So much of any contract as requires a purveyor of milk, on a sample of milk being procured under this Act—

    (*a*) to send to the person from whom he obtained the milk any part of that sample, or

    (*b*) to give to that person notice that a sample has been so procured,

shall be void.

(4) It is a defence for a person charged with an offence under this Act, or regulations made under this Act, in respect of a sample of milk taken after the milk has left his possession, to prove—

    (*a*) that the churn or other vessel in which the milk was contained was effectively closed and sealed at the time when it left his possession ; and

    (*b*) that it had been opened before the person by whom the sample was taken had access to it.

Sampling powers of Minister's inspectors.

82. The powers of sampling officers to take samples under section 78 may be exercised also, in relation to milk—

    (*a*) in any case, by an inspector of the Minister, and

    (*b*) for purposes connected with the enforcement of any provisions which, by virtue of section 74, are enforceable by the Minister, by an authorised officer of his,

and references to a sampling officer in section 78(6), in section 80, and in Part I of Schedule 7, shall be construed accordingly.

83.—(1) The Minister may, in relation to any matter appearing to him to affect the general interests of consumers or the general interests of agriculture in the United Kingdom, direct an officer of his department to procure samples of any specified food, and upon that direction the officer shall have all the powers of a sampling officer, and this Act shall apply as if he were a sampling officer, except that—

    (*a*) if he intends to submit any sample procured by him to be analysed, he shall divide it into four parts, and shall deal with three of those parts in the manner directed by Part I of Schedule 7, and send the fourth part to the Minister ; and

    (*b*) any fee for analysis shall be payable to the analyst by the food and drugs authority of the area in which the sample is procured.

(2) The Minister shall communicate the result of the analysis of any such sample to the food and drugs authority, and upon that communication the authority shall have the like duty to cause proceedings to be taken as if one of their officers had procured the sample and sent it to be analysed.

84. Where a person procures a sample consisting of a food or substance contained in unopened containers, and the division into parts of the food or substance contained in those containers—

    (*a*) is not reasonably practicable, or

    (*b*) might affect the composition, or impede the proper analysis, of the contents,

the provisions of Part I of Schedule 7, or of section 83, as the case may be, with respect to the division of samples into parts shall be deemed to be complied with if the person procuring the sample divides the containers into the requisite number of lots and deals with each lot as if it were a part in the manner provided by those provisions ; and references in this Act to a part of a sample shall be construed accordingly.

85. A local authority may, at the request of a person who has in his possession any food which has not been sold and is not intended for sale, and on payment by that person of such fee, if any, as may be fixed by the authority, arrange to have the food examined.

86. Every public analyst shall, as soon as may be after the last day of March, of June, of September and of December in every year, report to the authority by whom he was appointed the number of articles which have been analysed by him under

Side notes:

PART VI

Minister's power of direction.

Where division not practicable.

Examination of food not for sale.

Quarterly reports of analysts.

PART VI

this Act in his capacity of public analyst for their area during the preceding quarter of a year and the result of each analysis.

Enforcement

Power to
enter
premises.

87.—(1) An authorised officer of a council shall, on producing, if so required, some duly authenticated document showing his authority, have a right to enter any premises at all reasonable hours—

(a) for the purpose of ascertaining whether there is or has been on, or in connection with, the premises any contravention of the provisions of this Act or of any regulations or byelaws made under it, being provisions which the council are required or empowered to enforce, and

(b) generally for the purpose of the performance by the council of their functions under this Act or any such regulations or byelaws,

but admission to any premises used only as a private dwelling-house shall not be demanded as of right unless 24 hours' notice of the intended entry has been given to the occupier.

(2) If a justice of the peace, on sworn information in writing—

(a) is satisfied that there is reasonable ground for entry into any premises for any such purpose as is mentioned above, and

(b) is also satisfied either—

(i) that admission to the premises has been refused, or a refusal is apprehended and that notice of the intention to apply for a warrant has been given to the occupier, or

(ii) that an application for admission, or the giving of such a notice, would defeat the object of the entry, or that the case is one of urgency, or that the premises are unoccupied or the occupier temporarily absent,

the justice may by warrant signed by him authorise the council by any authorised officer to enter the premises, if need be by force.

(3) An authorised officer entering any premises by virtue of this section, or of a warrant issued under it, may take with him such other persons as may be necessary, and on leaving any unoccupied premises which he has entered by virtue of such a warrant shall leave them as effectively secured against trespassers as he found them.

(4) Every warrant granted under this section shall continue in force for a period of one month.

(5) If any person who, in compliance with this section, or of a warrant issued under it, is admitted into a factory or workplace discloses to any person any information obtained by him in the factory or workplace with regard to any manufacturing process or trade secret, he shall, unless the disclosure was made in the performance of his duty, be liable to a fine not exceeding level 3 on the standard scale or to imprisonment for a term not exceeding three months.

(6) Nothing in this section authorises any person, except with the permission of the local authority under the Animal Health Act 1981, to enter any cowshed or other place—

> (*a*) in which an animal affected with any disease to which that Act applies is kept ; and
>
> (*b*) which is situated in a place declared under that Act to be infected with such a disease.

88.—(1) An authorised officer of a council shall, on producing, if so required, some duly authenticated document showing his authority, have a right at all reasonable hours—

> (*a*) to enter any ship or aircraft for the purpose of ascertaining whether there is in the ship or aircraft any food imported as part of the cargo in contravention of the provisions of regulations made under Part I, being provisions which the council are required or empowered to enforce ; and
>
> (*b*) to enter any vehicle, stall or place other than premises, or any home-going ship, for any purpose for which he is empowered under section 87 to enter premises.

(2) Subsections (2), (3) and (4) of section 87 apply in relation to any ship, aircraft, vehicle, stall or place which may be entered under the powers conferred by subsection (1) of this section as they apply in relation to premises, and as if any reference to the occupier of premises were a reference to the master, commander or other person in charge of the ship, aircraft, vehicle, stall or place.

89.—(1) An inspector or authorised officer of the Minister and an authorised officer of the Secretary of State, for the purpose of ascertaining whether there is or has been any contravention of the provisions of this Act or of any regulations or order made under it, being provisions which the Minister in question is required or empowered to enforce—

> (*a*) shall have the powers of entry specified in subsection (2) ; and

C

PART VI

(b) an inspector or authorised officer of the Minister shall have those powers for the purpose of taking any sample of milk under section 82.

(2) The powers of entry referred to in subsection (1) are the like powers of entry as are exercisable under section 87 or section 88 by an authorised officer of a council; and in relation to an inspector or officer to whom the subsection applies, the reference in section 87(2) to the council shall be construed as a reference to the Minister or the Secretary of State, as the case may be.

(3) For the purposes of any regulations made under section 13, this section and section 91(1) and (3) have effect as if the Minister as well as the local authority were empowered to enforce those regulations so far as they apply to slaughterhouses and knackers' yards.

Movement of imported food.

90.—(1) Without prejudice to any power of examining food which may be conferred by regulations made under Part I, an authorised officer of a port health authority into whose district any food has been imported with a view to sale for human consumption may give directions to the person in possession of the food prohibiting or restricting its removal or delivery—

(a) during any period not exceeding 48 hours; and

(b) if within that period the officer so requires, until that person has notified the officer of the name of the person to whom, and the address to or at which, he proposes to send or deliver the food.

(2) The power conferred by subsection (1) on an authorised officer of a port health authority is exercisable also, in relation to an area not forming part of a port health district, by an authorised officer of a local authority or county council.

(3) A person who fails to comply with any direction given under subsection (1), or who in a notification under it knowingly makes any misstatement, is guilty of an offence.

Obstruction.

91.—(1) A person who wilfully obstructs any person acting in the execution of this Act, or of any regulation, byelaw, order or warrant made or issued under it, is liable to a fine not exceeding level 5 on the standard scale.

(2) If—

(a) a sampling officer applies to purchase any food or substance exposed for sale, or on sale by retail, and tenders the price for the quantity which he requires as a sample, and the person exposing the food or substance for sale, or having it for sale, refuses to bring the officer such quantity of it as mentioned above; or

(b) the seller or consignor of any article or substance of which an officer has power to take a sample, or a person having the charge for the time being of such an article or substance, refuses to allow the officer to take the quantity which he requires as a sample,

then, in any of the cases mentioned in those paragraphs, the person concerned shall be treated for the purposes of subsection (1) as having wilfully obstructed the officer; but where any food or substance is exposed for sale in an unopened container duly labelled, no person shall be required to sell it except in the unopened container in which it is contained.

(3) A person who—

    (a) fails to give to any person acting in the execution of this Act, or of any regulation, byelaw, order or warrant made or issued under it, any assistance which that person may reasonably request him to give, or

    (b) fails to give any information which that person is expressly authorised by this Act to call for or may reasonably require, or

    (c) when required to give any such information, knowingly makes any misstatement in respect of it,

is liable to a fine not exceeding level 5 on the standard scale, except that nothing in this subsection shall—

    (i) apply to section 90(3);

    (ii) be construed as requiring a person to answer any question or give any information if to do so might incriminate him.

(4) Subsection (3) is without prejudice to so much of section 118 as enables regulations made under this Act, or an order made under section 5, to contain provisions for imposing penalties on persons offending against the regulations or order.

Legal proceedings

92.—(1) A person guilty of an offence to which this section applies is liable—

    (a) on summary conviction, to a fine not exceeding the statutory maximum; and

    (b) on conviction on indictment, to a fine or imprisonment for a term not exceeding 2 years or to both.

Offences triable either way.

(2) This section applies to any offence under this Act, except an offence—

    (a) under section 65, or

    (b) under any provision of this Act specified in section 93(3),

but in the case of an offence under section 5(3) the liability

PART VI   under paragraph (*a*) of subsection (1) of this section includes a term of imprisonment not exceeding 3 months, or both such a term and the fine mentioned in that paragraph.

Summary offences.

93.—(1) Any offence to which this section applies is triable summarily.

(2) The offences to which this section applies are—

    (*a*) an offence under any provision of this Act specified in subsection (3);

    (*b*) an offence under regulations made under this Act other than an offence which by virtue of the regulations is triable either summarily or on indictment;

    (*c*) an offence under byelaws made under this Act;

    (*d*) an offence under an order made under section 5.

(3) The provisions of this Act mentioned in paragraph (*a*) of subsection (2) are—

         (*a*) section 18(4);

         (*b*) section 27(1);

         (*c*) section 28(1);

         (*d*) section 28(3);

         (*e*) section 31(1);

         (*f*) section 53(4);

         (*g*) section 56(1);

         (*h*) section 58;

         (*j*) section 87(5);

         (*k*) section 91(1); and

         (*l*) section 91(3).

(4) This section applies to Northern Ireland so far as it relates to those regulations and orders made under Part I which apply to Northern Ireland, and to the enforcement and execution of those regulations and orders.

Offences by corporations.

94.—(1) Where an offence under this Act, or any regulations or order made under this Act, which has been committed by a body corporate is proved to have been committed with the consent or connivance of, or to be attributable to any neglect on the part of—

    (*a*) any director, manager, secretary or other similar officer of the body corporate, or

    (*b*) any person who was purporting to act in any such capacity,

he as well as the body corporate shall be deemed to be guilty of that offence and shall be liable to be proceeded against and punished accordingly.

(2) In subsection (1) " director ", in relation to any body cor- PART VI
porate established by or under any enactment for the purpose of
carrying on under national ownership any industry or part of
an industry or undertaking, being a body corporate whose affairs
are managed by its members, means a member of that body
corporate.

95.—(1) No prosecution for an offence under this Act or Prosecutions.
regulations made under this Act which is triable either summarily or on indictment shall be begun after the expiry of—

    (a) three years from the commission of the offence, or

    (b) one year from its discovery by the prosecutor,

whichever is the earlier.

(2) Where a sample has been procured under this Act, no prosecution in respect of the article or substance sampled shall be
begun after the expiry of—

    (a) 28 days, in the case of a sample of milk,

    (b) two months, in any other case,

beginning with the date on which the sample was procured.

(3) Subsection (2) does not apply where the justice of
the peace before whom the information is laid certifies that he
is satisfied on oath that having regard to the circumstances of
the particular case it was not practicable to lay the information at an earlier date ; but a prosecution in respect of a sample
of milk shall not in any case be begun after the expiry of 42
days beginning with the date on which the sample was procured.

(4) Where a sample has been procured under this Act, any proceedings in respect of the article or substance sampled shall be
taken before a court having jurisdiction in the place where the
sample was procured ; but—

    (a) where a sample procured within one area is for the pur-
        poses of this Act deemed to have been procured within
        another area, proceedings may, at the prosecutor's
        option, be taken either before a court having jurisdic-
        tion in the area within which the sample was procured,
        or before a court having jurisdiction in the area within
        which it is deemed to have been procured ; and

    (b) where the article or substance sampled was sold and
        actually delivered to the purchaser, proceedings may, if
        the prosecutor so elects, be taken before a court having
        jurisdiction at the place of delivery.

(5) In any proceedings under this Act in respect of an article
or substance sampled—

    (a) the summons shall not be made returnable less than 14
        days from the day on which it is served ; and

PART VI

(b) a copy of any certificate of analysis obtained on behalf of the prosecutor, and of any certificate given by a justice under subsection (3), shall be served with the summons.

(6) In any proceedings under this Act, where a sample has been procured in such circumstances that its division into parts is required by this Act, the part of the sample retained by the person who procured it shall be produced at the hearing.

(7) Any regulations or order made under this Act and extending to Northern Ireland shall provide for applying, in relation to offences under them, the provisions—

(a) of this section, or

(b) of any corresponding Northern Ireland enactment,

subject to any such modifications or adaptations as may be specified in the regulations or order.

(8) Notwithstanding subsection (1), a person is not liable to be prosecuted for an offence under this Act or regulations made under this Act which was committed before 1st January 1983.

Proceedings by Government departments and councils.

96.—(1) Without prejudice to their powers of enforcement under any provision of this Act—

(a) the authorities specified in the first column of Schedule 8 may, where they are of opinion that the general interests of consumers are affected, institute proceedings for any of the offences specified in relation to them respectively in the second column of that Schedule ; but,

(b) except as otherwise expressly provided by this Act, proceedings shall not be instituted by any of those authorities for an offence against any such provisions of this Act, or of any regulations made under it, which it is the duty of any council to execute and enforce.

(2) A food and drugs authority or a local authority may institute proceedings under any section of, or any regulations made under, this Act if, and only if, they are the authority charged with its execution and enforcement, except that a local authority may institute proceedings under section 2 if the offence alleged relates to food which is alleged to contain some extraneous matter.

Evidence of analysis.

97.—(1) In any proceedings under this Act, the production by one of the parties—

(a) of a document purporting to be a certificate of a public analyst in the form prescribed under section 79(5), or

(b) of a document supplied to him by the other party as being a copy of such a certificate.

shall be sufficient evidence of the facts stated in it, unless, in the
first-mentioned case, the other party requires that the analyst
shall be called as a witness.

(2) In any such proceedings, if a sample of milk has been
taken by an officer of one authority at the request of an officer
of another authority, a document—

  (*a*) which purports to be a certificate signed by the officer
    who took the sample, and

  (*b*) which states that the provisions of this Act with respect
    to the manner in which samples are to be dealt with
    were complied with,

shall, if a copy of it has been served on the defendant with the
summons, be sufficient evidence of compliance with those provisions, unless the defendant requires that the officer shall be
called as a witness.

(3) In any such proceedings, if a defendant intends—

  (*a*) to produce a certificate of a public analyst, or

  (*b*) under subsection (1), to require that a public analyst
    shall be called as a witness, or

  (*c*) under subsection (2), to require that a sampling officer
    shall be called as a witness,

notice of his intention, together, in the first-mentioned case, with
a copy of the certificate, shall be given to the other party
at least three clear days before the day on which the summons
is returnable, and, if this requirement is not complied with, the
court may, if it thinks fit, adjourn the hearing on such terms as
it thinks proper.

(4) Regulations made under section 4 or section 7 may prescribe a method of analysis for the purpose of ascertaining the
presence in, or absence from, any food of any substance specified
in the regulations, or the quantity of any such substance which
is present in any food ; and in any proceedings under this Act—

  (*a*) for a contravention of any regulations made under either
    of those sections, or

  (*b*) for an offence under section 2 or section 6,

in respect of any food alleged to contain, or not to contain, any
substance specified as mentioned above, or any particular
quantity of such a substance, evidence of an analysis carried
out by the prescribed method shall be preferred to evidence of
any other analysis or test.

(5) Subsection (4) applies to Northern Ireland so far as it
relates—

  (*a*) to those regulations and orders made under Part I which
    apply to Northern Ireland, and

PART VI   (*b*) to the enforcement and execution of those regulations and orders,

and accordingly that subsection is modified by the omission of the words " under this Act " and paragraph (*b*).

Presumptions.   **98.** For the purposes of this Act and of any regulations or byelaws made under this Act—

(*a*) any article commonly used for human consumption shall, if sold or offered, exposed or kept for sale, be presumed, until the contrary is proved, to have been sold or, as the case may be, to have been or to be intended for sale, for human consumption ;

(*b*) any article commonly used for human consumption which is found on premises used for the preparation, storage, or sale of that article and any article commonly used in the manufacture of products for human consumption which is found on premises used for the preparation, storage or sale of those products, shall be presumed, until the contrary is proved, to be intended for sale, or for manufacturing products for sale, for human consumption ;

(*c*) any substance capable of being used in the composition or preparation of any article commonly used for human consumption which is found on premises on which that article is prepared shall, until the contrary is proved, be presumed to be intended for such use.

Analysis by Government Chemist.   **99.**—(1) The court before which any proceedings are taken under this Act may, if it thinks fit, and upon the request of either party shall, cause the part of any sample produced before the court under section 95(6) to be sent to the Government Chemist, who shall—

(*a*) make an analysis, and

(*b*) transmit to the court a certificate of its result,

and the costs of the analysis shall be paid by the prosecutor or the defendant as the court may order.

(2) If, in a case where an appeal is brought, no action has been taken under subsection (1), its provisions shall apply also in relation to the court by which the appeal is heard.

(3) Any certificate of the results of an analysis transmitted by the Government Chemist under this section shall be signed by or on behalf of the Government Chemist, but—

(*a*) the analysis may be made by any person acting under the direction of the person by whom the certificate is signed ; and

(b) any certificate so transmitted by the Government Chemist shall be evidence of the facts stated in it unless any party to the proceedings requires that the person by whom it is signed shall be called as a witness.

100.—(1) A person against whom proceedings are brought under this Act shall—

(a) upon information duly laid by him, and

(b) on giving to the prosecution not less than three clear days' notice of his intention,

be entitled to have any person to whose act or default he alleges that the contravention of the provisions in question was due brought before the court in the proceedings ; and—

(i) if, after the contravention has been proved, the original defendant proves that the contravention was due to the act or default of that other person, that other person may be convicted of the offence ; and

(ii) if the original defendant further proves that he has used all due diligence to secure that the provisions in question were complied with, he shall be acquitted of the offence.

(2) Where a defendant seeks to avail himself of the provisions of subsection (1)—

(a) the prosecution, as well as the person whom the defendant charges with the offence, shall have the right to cross-examine him, if he gives evidence, and any witness called by him in support of his pleas, and to call rebutting evidence ;

(b) the court may make such order as it thinks fit for the payment of costs by any party to the proceedings to any other party to them.

(3) Where—

(a) it appears to the authority concerned that an offence has been committed in respect of which proceedings might be taken under this Act against some person, and

(b) the authority are reasonably satisfied that the offence of which complaint is made was due to an act or default of some other person and that the first-mentioned person could establish a defence under subsection (1),

they may cause proceedings to be taken against that other person without first causing proceedings to be taken against the first-mentioned person.

In any such proceedings the defendant may be charged with, and, on proof that the contravention was due to his act or

PART VI   default, be convicted of, the offence with which the first-mentioned person might have been charged.

Contravention in Scotland or Northern Ireland.

101.—(1) Where proceedings are brought against any person (" the defendant ") in respect of a contravention of any provision of this Act, or of regulations made under this Act, and it is proved—

(a) that the contravention was due to the act or default of some other person, being an act or default which took place in Scotland or Northern Ireland, and

(b) that the defendant used all due diligence to secure compliance with those provisions,

the defendant shall, subject to subsection (2), be acquitted of the offence.

(2) The defendant shall not be entitled to be acquitted under this section unless within seven days from the date of the service of the summons on him he has given written notice to the prosecution of his intention to rely upon the provisions of this section, specifying the name and address of the person to whose act or default he alleges that the contravention was due, and has sent a like notice to that person.

(3) The person specified in a notice served under this section shall be entitled to appear at the hearing and to give evidence, and the court may, if it thinks fit, adjourn the hearing to enable him to do so.

(4) Where it is proved that the contravention of the provisions in question was due to the act or default of some person other than the defendant, being an act or default which took place in Scotland or Northern Ireland, the court shall (whether or not the defendant is acquitted) cause notice of the proceedings to be sent to the Minister.

Warranty pleaded as defence.

102.—(1) In any proceedings for an offence under this Act, or any regulations made under this Act, being an offence consisting of selling, or offering, exposing or advertising for sale, or having in possession for the purpose of sale, any article or substance, it is a defence for the defendant to prove—

(a) that he purchased it as being an article or substance which could lawfully be sold or otherwise dealt with as mentioned above, or, as the case may be, could lawfully be so sold or dealt with under the name or description or for the purpose under or for which he sold or dealt with it, and with a written warranty to that effect ; and

(b) that he had no reason to believe at the time of the commission of the alleged offence that it was otherwise ; and

(c) that it was then in the same state as when he purchased it.

PART VI

(2) A warranty is only a defence in proceedings under this Act if—

(a) the defendant—

(i) has, not later than three clear days before the date of the hearing, sent to the prosecutor a copy of the warranty with a notice stating that he intends to rely on it and specifying the name and address of the person from whom he received it, and

(ii) has also sent a like notice of his intention to that person, and

(b) in the case of a warranty given by a person resident outside the United Kingdom, the defendant proves that he had taken reasonable steps to ascertain, and did in fact believe in, the accuracy of the statement contained in it, and

(c) in the case of a prosecution in respect of a sample of milk procured from him, the defendant either—

(i) has within 60 hours after the sample was procured served such a notice as is mentioned in paragraph 12 of Schedule 7, or

(ii) not having served such a notice, proves that he had reasonable cause to believe that such a notice would have been of no effect by reason of the fact that the milk in question was a mixture of milk produced on more than one dairy farm.

(3) Where the defendant is a servant of the person who purchased the article or substance under a warranty, he shall be entitled to rely on the provisions of this section in the same way as his employer would have been entitled to do if he had been the defendant.

(4) The person by whom the warranty is alleged to have been given shall be entitled to appear at the hearing and to give evidence, and the court may, if it thinks fit, adjourn the hearing to enable him to do so.

(5) For the purposes of this section and section 103, a name or description entered in an invoice shall be deemed to be a written warranty that the article or substance to which the entry refers can be sold or otherwise dealt with under that name or description by any person without contravening any of the provisions of this Act or of regulations made under this Act.

103.—(1) A defendant who in any proceedings under this Act wilfully applies to any article or substance a warranty or certificate of analysis given in relation to any other article or substance is guilty of an offence.

Offences as to warranties and analysis certificates.

(2) A person who—

    (a) sells an article or substance in respect of which a warranty might be pleaded under section 102, and

    (b) gives to the purchaser a false warranty in writing in respect of that article or substance,

is guilty of an offence, unless he proves that when he gave the warranty he had reason to believe that the statements or description contained in it were accurate.

(3) Where the defendant in a prosecution under this Act relies successfully on a warranty given to him or to his employer, any proceedings under subsection (2) in respect of the warranty may at the prosecutor's option be taken either—

    (a) before a court having jurisdiction in the place where a sample of the article or substance to which the warranty relates was procured ; or

    (b) before a court having jurisdiction in the place where the warranty was given.

Appeals

Appeals to
magistrates'
courts.
1980 c. 43.

104.—(1) Where this Act or any regulations made under this Act provide for an appeal to a magistrates' court against a refusal or other decision of an authority, the procedure shall be by way of complaint for an order, and the Magistrates' Courts Act 1980 applies to the proceedings.

(2) The time within which such an appeal may be brought shall be 21 days from the date on which notice of the authority's refusal or other decision was served upon the person desiring to appeal, and for the purposes of this subsection the making of the complaint shall be deemed to be the bringing of the appeal.

(3) In any case where such an appeal lies, the document notifying to the person concerned the authority's decision in the matter shall state—

    (a) the right of appeal to a magistrates' court ; and

    (b) the time within which such an appeal may be brought.

Further
appeal to
Crown Court.

105. Where a person aggrieved by an order, determination or other decision of a magistrates' court under this Act, or under any regulation made under this Act, is not by any other enactment authorised to appeal to the Crown Court, he may appeal to such a court.

Effect of
court's
decision.

106. Where on an appeal under this Act, or under any regulations made under this Act, a court varies or reverses any decision of an authority, it is the authority's duty—

    (a) to give effect to the court's order ; and

(b) in particular, to grant any necessary licence and to make any necessary entry in any register.

107.—(1) Where a decision of an authority under this Act, or under any regulations made under this Act, refusing, cancelling, suspending or revoking, registration or a licence, or a decision of a magistrates' court on appeal against such a decision, makes it unlawful for a person—

> (a) to carry on any business which he, or his immediate predecessor in the business, was lawfully carrying on at the date when the decision of the authority was given, or

> (b) to use any premises for any purpose for which he, or his immediate predecessor in the business, was lawfully using them at that date,

he may carry on that business and use those premises for that purpose until the time for appealing has expired and, if an appeal is lodged, until the appeal is finally disposed of or abandoned or has failed for want of prosecution.

(2) The provisions of subsection (1) with respect to the right to continue to carry on a business and to use premises shall apply also where the decision of a court in proceedings in respect of an offence under this Act, or under any regulations made under this Act, makes it unlawful for a person—

> (a) to carry on a business which he was lawfully carrying on immediately before the decision was given ; or

> (b) to use any premises for any purpose for which he was then lawfully using them.

Compensation and arbitration

108. Where by Part I, except section 23, provision is made for the payment of compensation—

> (a) if the compensation claimed does not exceed £50, all questions as to the fact of damage or loss, and liability for and the amount of compensation, may on the application of either party be determined by, and any compensation awarded may be recovered before, a magistrates' court ;

> (b) in any other case, a dispute arising as to the fact of damage or loss, or as to the amount of compensation, shall be determined by arbitration under this Act.

109. In arbitrations under this Act the reference shall, except where otherwise expressly provided, be to a single arbitrator to be appointed by agreement between the parties, or, in default of agreement—

> (a) in relation to arbitrations under section 9(4) in respect

PART VI

of milk, or in respect of meat or meat products seized while in a slaughterhouse or in the course of importation, by the Minister ;

(b) in relation to other arbitrations, by the Secretary of State.

PART VII

GENERAL AND SUPPLEMENTAL

Acquisition of land, and order to permit works

Compulsory purchase of land.

110. A local authority may be authorised by the responsible Minister to purchase land compulsorily for the purposes of this Act, except for the purposes of paragraph (b) of section 50(1), and in relation to the compulsory purchase of land under this section—

1981 c. 67.

(a) the Acquisition of Land Act 1981 applies ; and

(b) " land " includes any interest in land and any easement or right in, to or over land.

In this section "the responsible Minister", in relation to the purposes of section 70, means the Minister, and in relation to the other purposes of this Act means the Secretary of State.

Order to occupier to permit works.

111. If, on a complaint made by the owner of any premises, it appears to a magistrates' court that the occupier of those premises prevents the owner from executing any work which he is by or under this Act required to execute, the court may order the occupier to permit the execution of the work.

In this section—

" owner " means the person for the time being receiving the rackrent of the premises, whether on his own account or as agent or trustee for any other person, or would so receive it if those premises were let at a rackrent ;

" premises " includes messuages, buildings, lands, easements and hereditaments of any tenure ;

" rackrent " means a rent which is not less than two thirds of the rent at which the property might reasonably be expected to let from year to year, free from all usual tenant's rates and taxes, and deducting from it the probable average annual cost of the repairs, insurance and other expenses (if any) necessary to maintain the property in a state to command such a rent.

Inquiries, and default

Local Inquiries.

112. The appropriate Minister may cause a local inquiry to be held in any case where he is authorised by this Act—

(a) to determine any difference,

(b) to make any order,

(c) to frame any scheme,

(d) to give any consent, confirmation, sanction or approval, or

(e) otherwise to act under this Act,

and in any other case where he deems it advisable that a local inquiry should be held in relation to any matter with which this Act is concerned in any place.

This section does not apply to Parts IV and V; and in this section "the appropriate Minister", in relation to anything authorised to be done under this Act by the Minister or the Ministers, or the Secretary of State, means that Minister or those Ministers, or the Secretary of State, as the case may be.

113.—(1) If—

(a) a complaint is made to the appropriate Minister that any council or joint board have failed to discharge their functions under this Act in any case where they ought to have done so, or

(b) the appropriate Minister is of opinion that an investigation should be made as to whether any council or joint board have failed as mentioned in paragraph (a),

the appropriate Minister may cause a local inquiry to be held into the matter.

(2) If, after a local inquiry has been held in pursuance of this section, the appropriate Minister is satisfied that there has been such a failure on the part of the council or board in question, he may make an order declaring them to be in default and directing them for the purpose of removing the default to discharge such of their functions, and in such manner and within such time or times, as may be specified in the order.

(3) If a council or board with respect to whom an order has been made under subsection (2) fail to comply with any requirement of the order within the time limited by it for compliance with that requirement, the appropriate Minister, instead of enforcing the order by mandamus or otherwise may—

(a) if the body in default are the council or a joint board whose district lies wholly within one county, or a port health authority whose district (so far as it does not consist of water) lies wholly within one county, make an order transferring to the council of the county such of the functions of the body in default as may be specified in his order;

(b) in any other case, make an order transferring to himself such of the functions of the body in default as may be so specified.

PART VII   (4) Where under this section the appropriate Minister has made an order transferring to a county council or to himself any functions of a council or joint board—

> (a) the appropriate Minister may by a subsequent order vary or revoke that order, but without prejudice to the validity of anything previously done under it ; and

> (b) when any order is so revoked the appropriate Minister may, either by the revoking order or by a subsequent order, provide as seems to him to be desirable with respect to the transfer, vesting and discharge of any property or liabilities acquired or incurred by the county council or by him in discharging any of the functions to which the order so revoked related.

(5) This section does not apply to Part IV ; and in this section " the appropriate Minister " means—

> (a) the Secretary of State, in relation to functions of councils or joint boards under any of the following provisions—

>> (i) sections 15, 16, 17, 18 and 19,
>> (ii) sections 27 and 28,
>> (iii) sections 30 and 31,
>> (iv) section 74, so far as it relates to the enforcement and execution of sections 8 and 9 (except in their application to milk, or to meat or to meat products while in a slaughterhouse or in the course of importation) and to the enforcement and execution of section 35 ;

> (b) the Secretary of State, in relation to functions of councils or joint boards under Part III ;

> (c) the Ministers, in relation to functions of councils or joint boards under regulations made under this Act ;

> (d) the Minister, in relation to any other functions of councils or joint boards.

Default: food and drugs authorities.   **114.** If the Minister, after communication with a food and drugs authority, is of opinion—

> (a) that the authority have failed in relation to any kind of food to execute or enforce any of the provisions of this Act which it is their duty to execute or enforce, and

> (b) that their failure affects the general interests of consumers, or the general interests of agriculture in the United Kingdom,

he may by order empower an officer of his department to execute and enforce, or procure the execution and enforcement of, those provisions in relation to that kind of food.

Nothing in this section affects any other power exercisable by the Minister or a county council with respect to defaults of local authorities.

115.—(1) Any expenses—

> (a) incurred by the appropriate Minister within the meaning of section 113 in discharging any functions of a council or joint board where he has by order under that section transferred those functions to himself, or
>
> (b) incurred by the Minister or his officer under section 114,

shall be paid in the first instance out of moneys provided by Parliament, but the amount of those expenses as certified by the appropriate Minister or the Minister, as the case may be, shall on demand be paid to him by the body in default, and shall be recoverable by him from them as a debt due to the Crown.

(2) For the purpose of raising the money so required the council or the joint board, or the food and drugs authority, as the case may be, shall have the like power as they have of raising money for defraying expenses incurred directly by them as such a council, board or authority.

(3) The payment of the expenses mentioned in subsection (1) shall to such extent as may be sanctioned by the Minister be a purpose for which a local authority, port health authority or joint board may borrow money in accordance with the statutory provisions relating to borrowing by such an authority or board.

Protection

116.—(1) An officer of a council is not personally liable in respect of any act done by him—

> (a) in the execution or purported execution of this Act, and
>
> (b) within the scope of his employment,

if he did that act in the honest belief that his duty under this Act required or entitled him to do it.

(2) Nothing in subsection (1) shall be construed as relieving a council from any liability in respect of the acts of their officers.

(3) Where—

> (a) an action has been brought against an officer of a council in respect of an act done by him in the execution or purported execution of this Act, and
>
> (b) the circumstances are such that he is not legally entitled to require the council to indemnify him,

the council may, nevertheless, indemnify him against the whole or a part of any damages and costs which he may have been ordered to pay or may have incurred, if they are satisfied—

(i) that he honestly believed that the act complained of was within the scope of his employment ; and

(ii) that his duty under this Act required or entitled him to do it.

(4) A public analyst appointed by a food and drugs authority shall for the purposes of this section be treated as being an officer of the authority whether or not he is employed whole-time.

Liability to rates no dis-qualification.

117. A judge of any court or a justice of the peace shall not be disqualified from acting in cases arising under this Act by reason only of his being as one of several ratepayers, or as one of any other class of persons, liable in common with the others to contribute to, or be benefited by, any rate or fund out of which any expenses of a council are to be defrayed.

Subordinate legislation

Certain regulations and orders.

118.—(1) Regulations made under Part I of this Act, Milk and Dairies Regulations and Milk (Special Designation) Regulations, may, without prejudice to the generality of the provisions under which they are made—

(a) modify for the purposes of the regulations any provision of this Act relating to the taking, analysis and examination of samples,

(b) apply, as respects matters to be dealt with by the regulations, any provision in any Act (including this Act) dealing with the like matters, with the necessary modifications and adaptations,

(c) (subject to paragraph 3 of Schedule 4) provide for an appeal to a magistrates' court against any refusal or other decision of an authority by whom the regulations are to be enforced and executed,

(d) authorise the making of charges for the purposes of the regulations, or for any services performed under them, and provide for the recovery of charges so made,

(e) provide that an offence under the regulations shall be triable either way,

(f) include provisions under which a person guilty of an offence under the regulations which is so triable is liable on summary conviction to a fine not exceeding the statutory maximum or such less amount as may be specified in the regulations and on conviction on indictment to either or both of the following—

(i) a fine not exceeding an amount specified in the regulations, or of an indefinite amount,

(ii) imprisonment for a term not exceeding two years or such shorter term as may be specified in the regulations,

(g) include provisions under which a person guilty of an offence under the regulations which is triable only summarily is liable on conviction to a fine not exceeding level 5 on the standard scale or such other level as may be specified in the regulations,

(h) make such ancillary and incidental provisions as appear to the Ministers to be necessary or desirable,

and regulations made under Part I, subject to such generality, may require persons carrying on any activity to which the regulations apply to keep and produce records and provide returns.

(2) Subsection (1), other than paragraphs (e) and (f), applies to an order made under section 5 as it applies to regulations made under Part I.

(3) The power conferred by paragraph (b) of subsection (1), in the case of Milk (Special Designation) Regulations, includes power, in dealing with the procuring of samples for the purpose of the enforcement of conditions of licences authorising the use of a special designation, to exclude provisions of Part II of Schedule 7 which may appear not to be appropriate for that purpose.

(4) Regulations made under section 13 or section 20, and any order made under section 17, may be made so as to apply throughout England and Wales or to apply only in such area or areas as may be specified in the regulations or order.

(5) Without prejudice to any other relevant power, any regulations made with respect to slaughterhouses or knackers' yards under section 13 may include provision for the regulations to come into force on different days fixed by, or by an order to be made under, those regulations in respect of different classes or descriptions of premises and different areas, and for different provisions to come into force on different days.

(6) Before making—

(a) any regulations to which subsection (1) applies, or

(b) an order under section 5 or section 17,

the Ministers shall consult with such organisations as appear to them to be representative of interests substantially affected by the regulations or by the order.

(7) Subsections (1), (2) and (6) apply to Northern Ireland so far as they relate—

(a) to those regulations and orders made under Part I which apply to Northern Ireland, or

PART VII

(*b*) to the enforcement and execution of those regulations and orders,

and in relation to Northern Ireland subsection (1) has effect subject to the following additional modifications—

(i) in paragraph (*a*), the reference to this Act includes a reference to any corresponding Northern Ireland enactment,

(ii) in paragraph (*b*), the reference to any Act includes a reference to any Northern Ireland enactment, and the reference to this Act includes a reference to any corresponding Northern Ireland enactment,

(iii) in paragraph (*c*), construe the reference to a magistrates' court as a reference to a court of summary jurisdiction,

and this section applies to Northern Ireland so far as it relates to an Order in Council made under section 133 and extending to Northern Ireland.

Community provisions.

119.—(1) The Ministers, as respects any directly applicable Community provision relating to food for which, in their opinion, it is appropriate to provide under this Act—

(*a*) may by regulations provide as they consider necessary or expedient for the purpose of securing that the Community provision is administered, executed and enforced under this Act; and

(*b*) may apply such of the provisions of this Act as may be specified in the regulations in relation to the Community provision with such modifications, if any, as may be so specified.

(2) For the purpose of complying with any Community obligation, or for conformity with any provision made for that purpose, the Ministers may by regulations provide as to—

(*a*) the manner of sampling any food specified in the regulations, and the manner in which samples are to be dealt with, and

(*b*) the method to be used in analysing, testing or examining samples of any food so specified,

and regulations made by the Ministers for that purpose, or for conformity with any provision so made, may modify or exclude any provision of this Act relating to the procuring or analysis of, or dealing with, samples or to evidence of the results of an analysis or test.

Statutory instruments.

120.—(1) Under this Act—

(*a*) any power to make regulations or orders, and

(*b*) the Secretary of State's power to make a declaration under section 16(5) or section 17(5),

is exercisable by statutory instrument, subject to section 4(2) PART VII
of the Agriculture Act 1967 in respect of an order made under 1967 c. 22.
section 57(2) of this Act.

(2) A statutory instrument containing—

(*a*) regulations made under Part I or Part II, or section 76(2), or section 119,

(*b*) an order made under section 5,

(*c*) an order made under section 43 ordering that section 40(1) shall cease to be in operation in any area, or an order under section 68, or

(*d*) an Order in Council made under section 133,

is subject to annulment in pursuance of a resolution of either House of Parliament.

(3) No order shall be made under section 17 unless a draft of it has been laid before Parliament and has been approved by resolution of each House.

(4) A draft of any statutory instrument containing an order made under section 43 bringing section 40(1) into operation in any area shall be laid before Parliament.

(5) In relation to Northern Ireland—

(*a*) subsection (1), and subsection (2) except paragraph (*c*), apply so far as they relate to regulations and orders made under Part I which apply to Northern Ireland, or to the enforcement and execution of those regulations and orders ; and

(*b*) this section applies so far as it relates to an Order in Council made under section 133 which extends to Northern Ireland.

121.—(1) The confirming authority in respect of byelaws Byelaws.
made under this Act is the Secretary of State.

(2) An authority who propose to apply to the Secretary of State for confirmation of any byelaws made under section 15 shall, in addition to complying with any other statutory requirements, publish in the London Gazette, at least one month before the application is made, notice of their intention to apply for confirmation.

(3) In so far as any byelaws made under this Act conflict with regulations made under Part I, the regulations shall prevail.

PART VII
Notices.

Notices, forms and continuances

122. All notices, orders, consents, demands and other documents authorised or required by or under this Act to be given, made or issued by a council, and all notices and applications authorised or required by or under this Act to be given or made to, or to any officer of, a council shall be in writing.

Power to
prescribe
documents.

123. The appropriate Minister may by regulations prescribe the form of any notice, advertisement, certificate or other document to be used for any of the purposes of this Act and, if forms are so prescribed, those forms or forms to the like effect may be used in all cases to which those forms are applicable.

In this subsection " appropriate Minister "—

(a) in relation to the purposes of sections 15, 16, 17, 18 and 19 and sections 28 and 31, means the Secretary of State ;

(b) in relation to the purposes of Part III, means the Secretary of State ; and

(c) in relation to other purposes, means the Minister.

Authentica-
tion.

124.—(1) Any notice, order, consent, demand or other document which a council are authorised or required by or under this Act to give, make or issue may be signed on behalf of the council—

(a) by the proper officer of the council as respects documents relating to matters within his province ; or

(b) by any officer of the council authorised by them in writing to sign documents of the particular kind or, as the case may be, the particular document.

(2) Any document purporting to bear the signature of an officer—

(a) expressed to hold an office by virtue of which he is under this section empowered to sign such a document, or

(b) expressed to be duly authorised by the council to sign such a document or the particular document,

shall for the purposes of this Act, and of any byelaws and orders made under it, be deemed, until the contrary is proved, to have been duly given, made or issued by authority of the council.

In this subsection " signature " includes a facsimile of a signature by whatever process reproduced.

125. Any notice, order, consent, demand or other document which is required or authorised by or under this Act to be given to or served on any person may, in any case for which no other provision is made by this Act, be given or served either—

    (a) by delivering it to that person ; or

    (b) in the case of the proper officer of a council, by leaving it or sending it in a prepaid letter addressed to him, at either his residence or his office, and, in the case of any other officer of a council, by leaving it or sending it in a prepaid letter addressed to him, at his office ; or

    (c) in the case of any other person, by leaving it or sending it in a prepaid letter addressed to him, at his usual or last known residence ; or

    (d) in the case of an incorporated company or body, by delivering it to their secretary or clerk at their registered or principal office, or by sending it in a prepaid letter addressed to him at that office ; or

    (e) in the case of a document to be given to or served on a person as being the owner of any premises by virtue of the fact that he receives the rackrent of the premises as agent for another, or would so receive it if the premises were let at a rackrent, by leaving it, or sending it in a prepaid letter addressed to him, at his place of business ; or

    (f) in the case of a document to be given to or served on the owner or the occupier of any premises, if it is not practicable after reasonable inquiry to ascertain the name and address of the person to or on whom it should be given or served, or if the premises are un-occupied, by addressing it to the person concerned by the description of " owner " or " occupier " of the premises (naming them) to which it relates, and—

        (i) delivering it to some person on the premises ; or

        (ii) if there is no person on the premises to whom it can be delivered, by affixing it, or a copy of it, to some conspicuous part of the premises.

In this section, " owner ", " premises " and " rackrent " mean the same as in section 111.

126. Where a person dies—

    (a) who holds a licence, or

    (b) who is registered in respect of any premises,

under this Act or any regulations made under this Act, the licence or registration shall, unless previously revoked or can-

PART VII   celled, subsist for the benefit of his personal representative, or his widow or any other member of his family—

    (i) until the expiry of two months from his death, or

    (ii) until the expiry of such longer period as the licensing or registering authority may allow.

Expenses and receipts

Meat inspection expenses.

127. In the cases mentioned below the Minister may by regulations approved by the Treasury provide for the making by him of contributions towards expenses incurred by a local authority in carrying out at slaughterhouses their functions with respect to the inspection of meat prepared for sale for human consumption.

The cases referred to above are those where the Minister is satisfied that, by reason of the extent to which the meat appears to him to exceed in quantity what it appears to him should be regarded as required for consumption in the authority's district, those expenses impose an unduly heavy burden on the ratepayers of that district.

Receipts under s. 44.

128. Any payments received by the Minister—

    (*a*) for milk sold by him under section 44, or

    (*b*) for treating under that section milk of others,

shall be paid into the Consolidated Fund.

County council expenses.

129.—(1) Expenses incurred by a county council as a food and drugs authority shall, if the council are not the food and drugs authority for the whole county, be defrayed as expenses for special county purposes charged on those districts the councils of which are not food and drugs authorities.

(2) Any expenses incurred by a county council in the enforcement and execution of—

    (*a*) regulations made under Part I,

    (*b*) Milk and Dairies Regulations, or

    (*c*) Milk (Special Designation) Regulations,

shall, if the Secretary of State by order so directs, be defrayed as expenses for special county purposes charged on such part of the county as may be provided by the order.

(3) A county council may, as part of their expenses as a food and drugs authority, contribute towards any expenses incurred by the council of a district within the county, not being a food and drugs authority, in connection with—

    (*a*) the procuring and analysis or examination of samples, and

(b) the institution of proceedings,
under this Act.

130.—(1) Expenses incurred under this Act by a sampling officer in procuring samples and causing samples to be analysed shall be defrayed by the authority of which he is an officer.

Sampling officer's expenses.

(2) The expenses incurred by an officer in complying with a notice given to him under section 81(2) shall be borne by the authority whose officer gave the notice, and any dispute as to the amount of any such expenses shall be referred to and determined by the Secretary of State.

Interpretation and operation

131.—(1) In this Act, unless the context otherwise requires, " food " includes drink, chewing gum and other products of a like nature and use, and articles and substances used as ingredients in the preparation of food or drink or of such products, but does not include—

Interpretation: " food ".

   (a) water, live animals or birds ;

   (b) fodder or feeding stuffs for animals, birds or fish ; or

   (c) articles or substances used only as drugs.

(2) For the purposes of this Act, except section 16 and without prejudice to the provisions of section 47—

   (a) the supply of food, otherwise than by sale, at, in or from any place where food is supplied in the course of a business shall be deemed to be a sale of that food, and references to purchasing and purchasers shall be construed accordingly ; and

   (b) where in connection with any business in the course of which food is supplied the place where food is served to the customer is different from the place where the food is consumed, both those places shall be deemed to be places in which food is sold.

132.—(1) In this Act, unless the context otherwise requires, and without prejudice to section 47—

Interpretation: further provision.

   " advertisement " includes any notice, circular, label, wrapper, invoice or other document, and any public announcement made orally or by any means of producing or transmitting light or sound, and " advertise " shall be construed accordingly ;

   " analysis " includes micro-biological assay but no other form of biological assay, and " analyse " shall be construed accordingly ;

" animal " does not include bird or fish ;

" area ", in relation to a county council and to officers of such a council, means, as the case may require, either the county or that part of the county for which the council are the food and drugs authority, and, in relation to a local authority and to officers of such an authority, means their district ;

" article " does not include a live animal or bird ;

" authorised officer " has the meaning given by section 73(1) ;

" business " includes the undertaking of a canteen, club, school, hospital or institution, whether carried on for profit or not, and any undertaking or activity carried on by a public or local authority ;

" catering premises " means premises where, in the course of a business, food is prepared and supplied for immediate consumption on the premises ;

" cheese " means the substance usually known as cheese, containing no fat other than fat derived from milk ;

" closure order " is an order within the meaning of section 21 ;

" container " includes any basket, pail, tray, package or receptacle of any kind, whether open or closed ;

" council " includes a port health authority ;

" cream " means that part of milk rich in fat which has been separated by skimming or otherwise ;

" dairy ", " dairy farm ", " dairy farmer " and " dairyman " have the meanings given by section 32 ;

" district ", in relation to a local authority, the City of London or the Inner or Middle Temple, and in relation to the officers of such an authority, means the area for which the authority acts ;

" drug " includes medicine for internal or external use ;

" emergency order " is an order within the meaning of section 22 ;

" food and drugs authority " has the meaning given by section 71 ;

" functions " includes powers and duties ;

" home-going ship " means a ship plying exclusively in inland waters, or engaged exclusively in coastal excursions ; and for the purpose of this definition " inland waters " means any canal, river, lake, navigation or estuary, and " coastal excursion " means an excursion lasting not more than one day which starts and ends in Great Britain and does not involve calling at any place outside Great Britain ;

" human consumption " includes use in the preparation of food for human consumption ;

" ice-cream " includes any similar commodity ;

" importation " has the same meaning as it has for the purposes of the Customs and Excise Management Act 1979, and " import " shall be construed accordingly ;

" importer ", in relation to an imported article, includes any person who, whether as owner, consignor, consignee, agent or broker, is in possession of the article or in any way entitled to the custody or control of it ;

" knacker's yard " means any premises used in connection with the business of slaughtering, flaying or cutting up animals the flesh of which is not intended for human consumption ;

" local authority ", in sections 44 and 45 has the meaning given by those sections, and elsewhere in this Act has the meaning given by section 72 ;

" milk " includes cream and separated milk, but does not include dried milk or condensed milk ;

" Milk and Dairies Regulations " has the meaning given by section 33 ;

" Milk (Special Designation) Regulations " has the meaning given by section 38 ;

" the Minister " means the Minister of Agriculture, Fisheries and Food and the Secretary of State, acting jointly, except in paragraph (a) of section 5(1), section 37 so far as it relates to the Minister's power to appoint veterinary inspectors, sections 68(5), 83, 101(4), 114 and paragraph (b) of section 115(1), where it means the Minister of Agriculture, Fisheries and Food ;

" the Ministers " means the Minister of Agriculture, Fisheries and Food, the Secretary of State for Social Services, and the Secretary of State for Wales, acting jointly ;

" officer " includes servant ;

" premises " means a building or part of a building, and any forecourt, yard or place of storage used in connection with a building or part of a building, and includes, in relation to dairies and dairy farms, and the trade of dairyman or dairy farmer, any land other than buildings ;

PART VII

" preparation ", in relation to food, includes manufacture and any form of treatment, and " preparation for sale " includes packaging ; and " prepare for sale " shall be construed accordingly ;

" proper officer ", in relation to any purpose and to any council or to any area, means the officer appointed for that purpose by that council or for that area, as the case may be ;

" public analyst " has the meaning given by section 76 ;

" purveyor ", in relation to milk, includes any person who sells milk, whether wholesale or by retail ;

" raw milk " means milk which has not been treated by heat ;

" sampling officer " has the meaning given by section 78 ;

" sanitary convenience " means a closet, privy or urinal ;

" separated ", in relation to milk, includes skimmed ;

1968 c. 59.

" ship " includes any boat or craft, and a hovercraft within the meaning of the Hovercraft Act 1968, and " master " shall be construed accordingly ;

1950 c. 28.

" shop " has the same meaning as in the Shops Act 1950 ;

" slaughterhouse " means a place for slaughtering animals, the flesh of which is intended for sale for human consumption, and includes any place available in connection with such a place for the confinement of animals while awaiting slaughter there or for keeping, or subjecting to any treatment or process, products of the slaughtering of animals there ;

1982 c. 48.

" standard scale " has the meaning given by section 75 of the Criminal Justice Act 1982 ;

" statutory maximum " has the meaning given by section 74 of the Criminal Justice Act 1982 ;

" substance " includes a liquid ;

" transit " includes all stages of transit from the dairy, place of manufacture or other source of origin, to the consumer ;

" vessel " includes a receptacle of any kind, whether open or closed.

(2) All powers and duties conferred or imposed by this Act shall be deemed to be in addition to, and not in derogation of, any other powers and duties conferred or imposed by Act of Parliament, law or custom, and, subject to any repeal effected by, or other express provision of, this Act, all such other powers and duties may be exercised and shall be performed in the same manner as if this Act had not been passed.

133.—(1) Her Majesty may by Order in Council provide for the application to the Crown of such of the provisions of this Act and of any regulations or order made under this Act as may be specified in the Order, with such exceptions, adaptations and modifications as may be so specified.

(2) Without prejudice to the generality of subsection (1), an Order under this section may make special provision for the enforcement of any provisions applied by the Order, and, where any such provision imposes a liability on a person by reason that he is—

(*a*) the occupier or owner of premises, or

(*b*) the owner of a business, or

(*c*) the principal on whose behalf any transaction is carried out,

the Order may provide for the determination, in a case where the premises are occupied or owned, or the business is owned, by the Crown, or the transaction is carried out on behalf of the Crown, of the person who is to be treated as so liable.

(3) This section applies to Northern Ireland (except so far as it relates to functions of the Crown in respect of the Crown in right of Her Majesty's Government in Northern Ireland, or to property held on the Crown's behalf for the purposes of such Government); and in that application the reference in subsection (1) to this Act includes a reference to any corresponding Northern Ireland enactment, and the reference to regulations shall be construed accordingly.

134. Schedule 9 has effect as to its transitional and saving provisions, and, subject to that Schedule—

(*a*) the enactments specified in Schedule 10 have effect subject to the amendments consequent on this Act specified in that Schedule, and

(*b*) the enactments and orders specified in Schedule 11 (which include enactments which were spent before the passing of this Act) are repealed and revoked to the extent specified in the third column of that Schedule,

but nothing in this Act shall be taken as prejudicing the operation of sections 16 and 17 of the Interpretation Act 1978 (which relate to the effect of repeals).

135.—(1) This Act applies to Northern Ireland as provided by—

(*a*) section 4(5);

(*b*) section 5(5);

(*c*) section 7(3);

(d) section 13(10) ;

(e) section 74(4) ;

(f) section 93(4) ;

(g) section 95(7) ;

(h) section 97(5) ;

(j) section 118(7) ;

(k) section 120(5) ;

(l) section 133(3) ; and

(m) Schedules 9, 10 and 11, so far as they relate to provisions which apply to Northern Ireland.

(2) In the application of this Act to Northern Ireland as provided by the provisions mentioned in subsection (1)—

(a) any reference to—

(i) " the Minister " shall be construed as a reference to the Minister of Agriculture, Fisheries and Food, and

(ii) " the Ministers " shall be construed as a reference to the Secretary of State for the Home Department, the Secretary of State for Social Services and the Minister of Agriculture, Fisheries and Food, acting jointly ; and

(b) any reference to a council shall be construed as, and any reference to a food and drugs authority shall be construed as including, a reference to a district council.

(3) In the following provisions " Northern Ireland enactment " means any enactment for the time being in force in Northern Ireland—

(a) section 4(4) ;

(b) section 74(4) ;

(c) section 95(7) ;

(d) section 118(7) ; and

(e) section 133(3).

Citation, extent and commencement.

136.—(1) This Act may be cited as the Food Act 1984.

(2) The following provisions of this Act apply to Scotland—

(a) sections 68 and 69, and paragraph 6 of Schedule 9,

(b) Schedule 10, so far as it amends any enactment which applies to Scotland,

1956 c. 48.
1972 c. 68.

(c) Schedule 11, so far as it repeals the Sugar Act 1956, and section 7(3) and (4) of the European Communities Act 1972, but apart from those provisions this Act does not apply to Scotland.

(3) This Act applies to Northern Ireland only so far as is provided by section 135.

(4) This Act comes into force at the end of the period of three months beginning with the day on which it is passed.

SCHEDULES

Section 28.

SCHEDULE 1

DISEASES TO WHICH SECTION 28(1) APPLIES

Enteric fever (including typhoid and paratyphoid fevers).
Dysentery.
Diphtheria.
Scarlet fever.
Acute inflammation of the throat.
Gastro-enteritis.
Undulant fever.

Section 34.

SCHEDULE 2

REFUSAL AND CANCELLATION OF REGISTRATION OF DAIRYMEN, DAIRY FARMS AND DAIRY FARMERS

PART I

DAIRYMEN

1. If it appears to an authority by whom dairymen are registered in pursuance of Milk and Dairies Regulations, other than the Minister, that the public health is, or is likely to be, endangered by any act or default of a person who has applied to be, or, is so registered by the authority, being an act or default, committed whether within or without the authority's district, in relation to the quality, storage or distribution of milk, they may serve on him a notice—

   (a) stating the place and time, not being less than 21 days after the date of the service of the notice, at which they propose to take the matter into consideration ; and

   (b) informing him that he may attend before them, with any witnesses whom he desires to call, at the place and time mentioned, to show cause why they should not, for reasons specified in the notice, refuse to register him or cancel his registration, as the case may be, either generally or in respect of any specified premises.

2. A person entitled under paragraph 1 to appear before any authority—

   (a) may appear in person or by counsel or a solicitor or any other representative ; or

   (b) may be accompanied by any person he may wish to assist him in the proceedings.

3. If a person on whom a notice is served under paragraph 1 fails to show cause to the authority's satisfaction, they may refuse to

register him or may cancel his registration, as the case may be, and—

  (a) shall forthwith give notice to him of their decision in the matter; and

  (b) shall, if so required by him within 14 days from the date of their decision, give to him within 48 hours after receiving the requirement, a statement of the grounds of the decision.

4. A person aggrieved by the decision of an authority under this Part to refuse to register him, or to cancel his registration, may appeal to a magistrates' court.

5. The court before whom a person registered as a dairyman otherwise than by the Minister is convicted of an offence under any of the provisions relating to milk in this Act, or under Milk and Dairies Regulations, may, in addition to any other punishment, cancel his registration as such.

6. An authority other than the Minister may require a person who applies to them for registration as a dairyman to give to them, before his application is considered, information as to whether he is, or has been, registered as a dairyman, whether by them or the Minister or some other authority, and if an applicant who is so required gives to the authority any information which is false in any material respect, he is guilty of an offence.

7. Where under this Part a person's application for registration is refused, or his registration is cancelled, he shall not be liable for any breach of contract for the purchase of further supplies of milk from any person, if the refusal or cancellation was due to the quality of the milk supplied by that person.

PART II

DAIRY FARMS AND DAIRY FARMERS

8. Milk and Dairies Regulations shall provide—

  (a) for the refusal by the Minister of registration of a dairy farm or of a person carrying on, or proposing to carry on, the trade of a dairy farmer, if in his opinion, having regard to the conditions existing at the premises to be registered, the regulations cannot be complied with and the registration should be refused; and

  (b) for the cancellation of any such registration by the Minister if in his opinion the regulations are not being complied with and the registration should be cancelled.

9. Any regulations made by virtue of paragraph 8 shall—

  (a) require notice to be given to the person affected of any intention to refuse or cancel the registration, stating the grounds on which it is alleged that the regulations cannot be or are not being complied with, as the case may be,

D

and his rights of making objections and representations in accordance with the regulations ;

(*b*) enable that person, within the time prescribed by the regulations (which shall not be less, in the case of a refusal, than 28 days or, in the case of a cancellation, than 21 days, from the date of service of that notice) to object, in respect of all or any of the grounds stated in that notice, that the regulations can be or are being complied with, as the case may be ;

(*c*) provide for the reference of any such objection to a tribunal constituted in accordance with the regulations ;

(*d*) provide for the procedure of that tribunal, and in particular for entitling the person objecting to appear before the tribunal with any witnesses he desires to call, and to require the tribunal to inspect the premises to which the objections relate ;

(*e*) require that tribunal to determine whether the objections are made out and, if not, on which of the grounds in respect of which they are made they are not made out, and provide that, in the event of a difference of opinion among the members of the tribunal, the determination of the majority of them shall be the determination of the tribunal ;

(*f*) require that the determinations of the tribunal shall be reported to the Minister and communicated by him to the person objecting, and to provide that the determinations of the tribunal as stated in the report shall, for the purpose of the proposal to refuse or cancel registration, be conclusive evidence of the facts found by it ;

(*g*) enable that person within the time so prescribed to make representations to the Minister that the registration should not be refused or cancelled on the grounds stated in the notice mentioned in sub-paragraph (*a*) ;

(*h*) provide that no registration shall be cancelled—

    (i) in any case, until the expiry of the prescribed time for making objections or representations under the regulations ;

    (ii) in a case where an objection is made within that time, until the report of the tribunal on it has been received and considered by the Minister ;

    (iii) in a case where representations are made to the Minister within that time, until the representations have been considered by him.

10. There shall be paid out of moneys provided by Parliament to the chairman of any such tribunal as is referred to in paragraph 9 such remuneration (by way of salary or fees) and such allowances as the Minister may, with the Treasury's approval, determine.

SCHEDULE 3

DISEASES OF COWS TO WHICH SECTION 35 APPLIES

Acute Mastitis.

Actinomycosis of the udder.

Suppuration of the udder.

Any infection of the udder or teats which is likely to convey disease.

Any comatose condition.

Any septic condition of the uterus.

Anthrax.

Foot-and-mouth disease.

SCHEDULE 4

LICENCES TO USE SPECIAL DESIGNATIONS

PART I

GENERAL

1.—(1) Milk (Special Designation) Regulations shall enable—

(a) the licensing authority, or

(b) on appeal to him under this Schedule, the Minister,

to revoke or suspend a licence authorising the use of a special designation, on the ground of any breach of a condition of the licence proved to the licensing authority's satisfaction, or, as the case may be, to the Minister's.

(2) This paragraph has, in relation to licences for specified areas, effect subject to Part II.

2. Those regulations shall provide as to any decision to refuse or suspend or revoke such a licence—

(a) where the licensing authority is a local authority, for conferring on the applicant or the holder of the licence, as the case may be (in this Schedule called " the person affected ") a right to be heard by the appropriate committee of the authority before a decision is made, and a right of appeal to the Minister against a decision adverse to the person affected ;

(b) for requiring the Minister on any such appeal to him, and when acting as licensing authority, before making his decision to afford to the person affected an opportunity of making representations ;

(c) for securing that any such hearing by a committee shall be in public, that the person affected shall be entitled to be heard by himself or by counsel or a solicitor or other representative as he may elect, and that he or his representative shall be entitled to call witnesses and to cross-examine witnesses called by another ; and

(*d*) for securing that such notice of a decision or proposed decision shall be given to the person affected as may be requisite for enabling him effectively to exercise rights conferred on him by this paragraph.

3. Paragraph (*c*) of section 118(1) does not apply to any such decision as is mentioned in paragraph 2 above.

PART II

LICENCES HELD BY RETAILERS FOR SPECIFIED AREAS

4.—(1) Any provision for the revocation of a licence authorising the use of a special designation on the ground of breach of a condition of the licence made by Milk (Special Designation) Regulations shall be such as to secure that a licence held by a retailer for a specified area shall not be revoked, and a grant of a licence by way of renewal of a licence so held shall not be refused, on the ground of breach of a condition of the licence so held, unless—

(*a*) the breach in question is of a condition to which section 45 applies,

(*b*) the holder of the licence has been convicted of an offence under that section because of the breach in question, or has been convicted, within 12 months before the time of the breach in question or after the time of it, of an offence under section 39, section 40 or section 41, or of an offence under Milk and Dairies Regulations for which a penalty is imposed by those regulations ; and

(*c*) the decision of the licensing authority to revoke, or to refuse renewal, as the case may be, is made within 12 months from the date of the breach in question.

(2) Any provision for the suspension of a licence authorising the use of a special designation on the ground of breach of a condition of the licence made by Milk (Special Designation) Regulations shall be such as to secure that—

(*a*) a licence held by a retailer for a specified area shall not be suspended, by virtue of any one decision of the authority having power to suspend it, for a period of more than 3 months, but

(*b*) a period of suspension of such a licence awarded by any such decision may be extended by a subsequent such decision made in accordance with the provisions of this Schedule.

(3) For the purposes of any decision for the suspension of a licence held by a retailer for a specified area, the term of that licence and of any licence granted by way of its renewal shall be treated as if they had been a single term, and accordingly—

(*a*) a period of suspension of such a licence of 3 months or less may be awarded notwithstanding that that period is longer than the unexpired residue of the term of the licence ; and

(b) where such a longer period of suspension of such a licence is awarded, a licence may be granted by way of its renewal but that licence shall be in suspense until the expiry of that period, and such a decision for extension of that period as is mentioned in paragraph (b) of sub-paragraph (2) of this paragraph may be made so as to extend the suspension of that licence.

5. Paragraph 1, in so far as it relates to proof of a breach of condition of a licence, has effect subject as follows—

(a) the provision to be made as there mentioned extends to a breach because of which the holder of the licence has been convicted of an offence under section 45 without requiring any proof of the breach other than conviction ; and

(b) in relation to a case referred to a tribunal by virtue of the subsequent provisions of this Schedule, not being a case in which the holder of the licence has been convicted as mentioned above, paragraph 1 has effect with the substitution of a reference to proof by the finding of the tribunal for the reference to proof to the satisfaction of the licensing authority or the Minister.

6.—(1) Milk (Special Designation) Regulations shall, where the issue is as to the revocation or suspension of a licence held by a retailer for a specified area, or as to the refusal to grant such a licence by way of renewal of such a licence, provide—

(a) for requiring the Minister on such an appeal as is mentioned in sub-paragraph (a) of paragraph 2, and when acting as licensing authority, to refer the matter to a tribunal constituted in accordance with the regulations if the person affected so requests ;

(b) for requiring that the duty of such a tribunal on any such reference shall be—

(i) to report findings on any question of fact appearing to them to be relevant, and

(ii) in particular, where the issue is as to revocation or suspension on the ground of a breach of condition not being one because of which the holder of the licence has been convicted of an offence under section 45, to find and report whether the breach was in fact committed (which finding shall be conclusive for the purposes of this Schedule) ;

(c) for requiring the Minister to consider the report of the tribunal before making his decision ;

(d) for the procedure of such a tribunal, including provision for conferring on the person affected a right to be heard by the tribunal, and including provision for treating the finding of a majority of the members of such a tribunal as the finding of the tribunal in the event of a difference of opinion among the members ;

(e) for securing that any such hearing as mentioned above by a tribunal shall be in public, that the person affected shall be entitled to be heard by himself or by counsel or a solicitor or other representative as he may elect, and that he or his representative shall be entitled to call witnesses and to cross-examine witnesses called by another ; and

(f) for securing that such notice of a decision or proposed decision shall be given to the person affected as may be requisite for enabling him effectively to exercise rights conferred on him by virtue of the foregoing provisions of this paragraph.

(2) There shall be paid out of moneys provided by Parliament to the chairman of any such tribunal such remuneration (by way of salary or fees) and such allowances as the authority appointing him may, with the Treasury's approval, determine.

SCHEDULE 5

CONDITIONS TO WHICH SECTION 45 APPLIES

Conditions to which section 45 applies are conditions relating to any of the following matters—

1. The examination or testing of animals, the inoculation of animals, the keeping of any animal or herd away from other animals, or other measure for detecting the existence of disease in animals or preventing the contracting or spread of it.

2. The marking, or keeping of records, of any animals, or other measures for their identification.

3. The subjection of milk to any process of heat-treatment, or to any cooling or other process, requirements in connection with the subjection of milk to such a process or as to the temperature or other conditions under which it is to be kept afterwards, or the recording or retention of evidence of the observance of such requirements.

4. Satisfaction of a test of milk, being a test related to the subjection of milk to such a process as is mentioned above or to the observance of any such requirements as are mentioned above.

5. Measures for securing that milk produced, or subjected to a process, as required by any condition is kept away from, and free from admixture with, other milk not so produced or subjected or other things, or is not subjected to some specified process.

6. The manner in which milk produced, or subjected to any process, in accordance with any conditions is to be dealt with

or kept as respects the receptacles in which it is to be put or to SCH. 5 remain, the closing or fastening of receptacles, or the marking of receptacles, or of things by which they are closed or fastened.

7. The manner of describing milk produced, or subjected to any process, in accordance with any conditions.

8. The making or keeping of records of milk produced, bought, subjected to any process, or sold.

SCHEDULE 6

Section 74.

PROVISIONS OF THIS ACT TO BE ENFORCED BY PARTICULAR AUTHORITIES

Provisions to be enforced and executed by the Minister

1.—(1) Any order under section 5.

(2) Section 39, so far as it applies to anything done in relation to raw milk by the producer of the milk.

(3) Section 45(1), so far as it relates to—

    (a) licences authorising the use of a special designation in relation to milk by a local authority within the meaning of section 45 ; and

    (b) licences authorising the use of a special designation in relation to raw milk by the producer of the milk.

(4) Milk and Dairies Regulations in respect of—

    (a) dairy farms,

    (b) the registration of persons carrying on or proposing to carry on the trade of a dairy farmer, or

    (c) the registration of occupiers of premises used temporarily as dairy farms,

but excluding regulations made for the purposes of paragraph (f) or paragraph (g) of section 33(1).

(5) Milk (Special Designation) Regulations in respect of the use of a special designation of raw milk by the producer of the milk.

Provisions to be enforced and executed by food and drugs authorities

2.—(1) Sections 1, 2 and 6.

(2) Section 36, and regulations having effect as if made under 1955 c. 16. section 33 of the Food and Drugs Act 1955. (4 & 5 Eliz. 2)

(3) Section 39(1) and (2) (except as regards any use of a special designation in relation to raw milk, and as regards the making of any reference to raw milk by such a description as is mentioned in that subsection (2), by the producer of the milk) ;

(4) Sections 40, 41 and 48.

SCHEDULE 7

SAMPLING

PART I

MANNER IN WHICH SAMPLES TAKEN OR PURCHASED FOR ANALYSIS ARE TO BE DEALT WITH

1. The sampling officer shall forthwith divide the sample into three parts, each part to be marked and sealed or fastened up in such manner as its nature will permit, and shall—

   (a) with respect to one part of the sample comply with paragraphs 2 to 8, and

   (b) deal with the remaining parts in accordance with paragraph 9.

2.—(1) If the sample was purchased by the sampling officer, he shall give the part of the sample to the vendor.

   (2) In relation to a sample purchased from an automatic machine, this paragraph applies as if for the reference to the vendor there were substituted a reference—

   (a) if the name and address (being an address in England and Wales) of a person stated to be the proprietor of the machine appears on the machine, to that person ;

   (b) in any other case, to the occupier of the premises on which the machine stands or to which it is affixed.

3. If the sample is of goods consigned from outside England and Wales and was taken by the sampling officer before delivery to the consignee, the officer shall give the part of the sample to the consignee.

4.—(1) This paragraph applies in relation to any sample of milk taken by the sampling officer, except to—

   (a) one in relation to which paragraph 3 applies ; or

   (b) any sample of cream.

   (2) If the sample was taken from a container—

   (a) having a capacity greater than six pints, and

   (b) appearing to the officer to show the name and address (being an address in England and Wales) of any person as consignor of the milk,

the officer shall give the part of the sample to that person.

   (3) If the sample was taken from a container—

   (a) having a capacity of six pints or less, and

   (b) appearing to the officer to show the name and address (being an address in England and Wales) of any person as the person who put the milk into the container,

the officer shall give the part of the sample to that person.

(4) If—

> (*a*) neither sub-paragraphs (2) or (3) apply, and
>
> (*b*) the sample was taken at a dairy,

the officer shall give the part of the sample to the occupier of the dairy.

(5) If none of sub-paragraphs (2) to (4) apply, the officer shall give the part of the sample—

> (*a*) to the occupier of the dairy from which the milk was consigned ; or
>
> (*b*) if the milk was consigned from more than one dairy, to the occupier of the dairy from which it was last consigned.

5. If—

> (*a*) none of the foregoing paragraphs of this Schedule apply, and
>
> (*b*) the sample was taken by the sampling officer at the request of a purchaser, or taken with the consent of a purchaser by retail,

the officer shall give the part of the sample to the vendor.

6. If—

> (*a*) none of the foregoing paragraphs of this Schedule apply, and
>
> (*b*) the sample was taken in transit,

the sampling officer shall give the part of the sample to the consignor.

7. If none of the foregoing paragraphs of this Schedule apply, the sampling officer shall give the part of the sample to the person appearing to be the owner of the food or substance of which the sample was taken.

8. In every case to which paragraphs 2 to 7 apply the sampling officer shall inform the person to whom the part of the sample is given that the sample was purchased or taken for the purpose of analysis by a public analyst.

9. Of the remaining parts of the sample, the sampling officer shall, unless he decides not to have an analysis made, submit one for analysis in accordance with section 79, and retain the other for future comparison.

10. Any part of a sample which under this Schedule is to be given to any person may be given either by delivering it to him or to his agent or by sending it to him by registered post or the recorded delivery service ; but where after reasonable inquiry the sampling officer is unable to ascertain the name and address of the person to whom the part of the sample is to be given, he may, in lieu of giving the part to that person, retain it.

PART II

SPECIAL PROVISIONS AS TO SAMPLING OF MILK

11. Where a sample of milk is procured from a purveyor of milk, he shall, if required to do so by the person by whom or on whose behalf the sample was procured, state the name and address of the seller or consignor from whom he received the milk.

12.—(1) Within 60 hours after the sample was procured from the purveyor, he may serve on the authority by whose officer it was procured, or, if it was not procured by an officer of any authority, on the food and drugs authority within whose area it was procured, a notice—

    (a) stating the name and address of the seller or consignor from whom he received the milk and the time and place of delivery to himself of milk from a corresponding milking; and

    (b) requesting the authority to take immediate steps to procure, as soon as practicable, a sample of milk from a corresponding milking in the course of transit or delivery to himself from the seller or consignor.

(2) If such a sample has been so procured since the sample in question was procured, or had been so procured within 24 hours prior to that sample being procured, it is not necessary for the authority to procure another sample in accordance with the notice.

(3) The purveyor has no right to require that such a sample shall be procured if the milk from which the sample procured from him was taken was a mixture of milk produced on more than one dairy farm.

13. If a purveyor has served on the authority such a notice as is mentioned above, and the authority have, in a case not falling within paragraph 12(2) or (3), omitted to procure a sample of milk from the seller or consignor in accordance with the foregoing provisions, no proceedings under this Act shall be taken against the purveyor in respect of the sample procured from him.

14. Any sample so procured in the course of transit or delivery shall be submitted for analysis to the analyst to whom the sample procured from the purveyor is or was submitted.

15. If proceedings are taken against the purveyor, a copy of the certificate of the result of the analysis of every sample so procured in the course of transit or delivery shall be given to him, and every such certificate and copy shall, subject to section 97, be admissible as evidence on any question whether the milk sold by the purveyor was sold in the same state as it was when he purchased it.

16. The authority by whose officer, or within whose area, the first mentioned sample was procured may, instead of, or in addition

to, taking proceedings against the purveyor, take proceedings against
the seller or consignor.

17.—(1) If a sample of milk of cows in any dairy is procured in course of transit or delivery from that dairy, the dairyman may, within 60 hours after the sample was procured, serve on the authority by whose officer the sample was procured a notice requesting them to take immediate steps to procure as soon as practicable a sample of milk from a corresponding milking of the cows and, thereupon, paragraphs 12 to 15 shall, so far as applicable, apply with any necessary modifications.

(2) The person procuring the sample shall be empowered to take any such steps at the dairy as may be necessary to satisfy him that the sample is a fair sample of the milk of the cows when properly and fully milked.

SCHEDULE 8

Government Departments Specially Authorised to Institute Proceedings for Offences

Minister	Offences for which proceedings may be instituted
The Minister	An offence against section 1, section 2 or section 6; An offence against section 8 committed in respect of milk, or in respect of meat or meat products while in a slaughterhouse or in the course of importation; An offence against section 12; An offence against regulations mad by the Ministers under section 4 or section 7.
The Secretary of State.	An offence against section 8, other than an offence committed in respect of milk, or in respect of meat or meat products while in a slaughterhouse or in the course of importation; An offence against section 16, section 27 or section 31.

SCHEDULE 9

Transitional and Saving Provisions

Time running

1. Where a period of time specified in an enactment repealed by this Act is current at the Act's commencement, the Act has effect as if the provision corresponding to that enactment had been in force when that period began to run.

Section 41(1) *Food and Drugs Act* 1955

2. Subject to section 43(1), the provisions of section 40(1) of this Act shall be in operation in any area in which, immediately before the commencement of this Act, corresponding provisions were in operation by virtue of section 41(1) of the Food and Drugs Act 1955.

Local Acts

3.—(1) In section 303 of the Public Health Act 1875 (power to repeal and alter local Acts by provisional orders), the reference to any local Act which relates to the same subject-matters as that Act shall be construed as including a reference to any local Act which relates to the same subject-matters as this Act.

(2) Notwithstanding the repeal by this Act of the provisions of sections 131(2) and Part II of Schedule 9 to the Food and Drugs Act 1955, any application may be made and any power may be exercised in relation to those provisions as and to the extent that they were capable of being made and exercised immediately before the commencement of this Act.

(3) Any power exercisable under section 48 of the Local Government (Miscellaneous Provisions) Act 1982 (consequential repeal or amendment of local statutory provisions) in relation to a provision of that Act repealed by this Act is exercisable in relation to the corresponding provision of this Act as and to the extent that it was capable of such exercise immediately before the commencement of this Act.

Public Health (Shell-Fish) Regulations 1934

4. An order having effect immediately before the commencement of this Act under the Public Health (Shell-Fish) Regulations 1934—

(a) continues in force under those regulations of 1934 ; and

(b) may be further continued by regulations made under section 13 as if it had been made under such regulations.

Orders under Defence (Sale of Food) Regulations 1943

5.—(1) Any order made under regulation 2 of the Defence (Sale of Food) Regulations 1943, being an order which was in force immediately before the commencement of this Act, shall—

(a) in the case of an order made by the Minister of Food or by the Minister of Agriculture, Fisheries and Food for the purposes of paragraph (1)(a) of that regulation, continue in force and have effect as if contained in regulations made by the Ministers under section 7,

(b) in the case of an order made by the Minister of Food or by the Minister of Agriculture, Fisheries and Food for the purposes of paragraph (1)(b) of that regulation, continue in force and have effect as if contained in regulations made by the Ministers under section 4, and references in this Act to regulations made under those sections SCH. 9 shall be construed accordingly.

(2) Such an order may be varied or revoked accordingly by regulations made under section 4 or section 7, as the case may be ; and the order shall have effect, subject to any variation by regulations under this Act—

    (*a*) as if it provided that any breach was an offence under this Act ; and

    (*b*) as if it specified a food and drugs authority as the authority to enforce the provisions of the order within their area.

Sugar Act 1956

1956 c. 48.

6.—(1) Notwithstanding the repeal by this Act of section 23(4) of the Sugar Act 1956—

    (*a*) that subsection (which provides that British Sugar, public limited company, shall furnish the Minister and the Secretary of State with such estimates, returns, accounts and other information as to the company's business as they may respectively require) continues to have effect, and

    (*b*) the power under section 4 of, and Part II of Schedule 3 to, the European Communities Act 1972 in relation to the re- 1972 c. 68. peal of that subsection continues to be exercisable,

as if that subsection had not been repealed.

(2) Nothing in this Act affects the saving (as regards advances made and guarantees given before 1st February 1973) in relation to section 22 of the Sugar Act 1956 in Part II of Schedule 3 to the European Communities Act 1972.

Sections 252 *and* 254 *Local Government Act* 1972

1972 c. 70.

7. Section 252 (general power to adapt Acts and instruments) and section 254 (consequential and supplementary provision) of the Local Government Act 1972 have effect in relation to those provisions of this Act which reproduce enactments which were in force before 1st April 1974 as if those provisions had been in force before that date.

SCHEDULE 10

CONSEQUENTIAL AMENDMENTS

City of London (*Various Powers*) *Act* 1959

1959 c. xlix.

1. In section 10(3) of the City of London (Various Powers) Act 1959, for " Food and Drugs Act 1955 " substitute " Food Act 1984 ". 1955 c. 16 (4 & 5 Eliz. 2).

London County Council (*General Powers*) *Act* 1959

1959 c. lii

2. In section 13(3) of the London County Council (General Powers) Act 1959, for " Food and Drugs Act 1955 " substitute " Food Act 1984 ".

Public Health Act 1961

3. In paragraph (*b*) of section 41(1) of the Public Health Act 1961, for " subsection (1) of section twenty-three of the Food and Drugs Act 1955 " substitute " section 28(1) of the Food Act 1984 ".

Weights and Measures Act 1963

4. In sections 29(3) and 58(1) of the Weights and Measures Act 1963, for " Food and Drugs Act 1955 " substitute " Food Act 1984 ".

5. In paragraph 1(*e*) of Part I of Schedule 10 to that Act—

   (*a*) for " Food and Drugs Act 1955 " substitute " Food Act 1984 " ;

   (*b*) for " section 134 of, and Schedule 10 to " substitute " sections 7(3) and 135 of ".

London Government Act 1963

6. For subsection (1) of section 54 of the London Government Act 1963, substitute—

   " (1) The council of a London borough shall, as respects that borough, be the authority responsible for enforcing section 35 of the Food Act 1984 (which prohibits the sale of milk from diseased cows), and the Common Council shall, as respects the City, be the authority for enforcing that section 35 ; and in that Act of 1984—

   (*a*) Part III (which relates to the provision and regulation of markets) extends to all the London boroughs ; and

   (*b*) section 70 (which relates to cold storage) extends to the whole of Greater London.".

Agriculture Act 1967

7. In paragraph (*e*) of section 4(1) and in section 4(2) of the Agriculture Act 1967, for " section 56(2) of the Food and Drugs Act 1955 " substitute " section 57(2) of the Food Act 1984 ".

8. In section 7(3) of that Act, for " Food and Drugs Act 1955 " substitute " Food Act 1984 ".

9. In section 25(2) of that Act, for " section 135(1) of the Food and Drugs Act 1955 " substitute " section 132(1) of the Food Act 1984 ".

Farm and Garden Chemicals Act 1967

10. In subsections (3) and (7)(*c*) of section 4 of the Farm and Garden Chemicals Act 1967, for " section 89 of the Food and Drugs Act 1955 " substitute " section 76 of the Food Act 1984 ".

Trade Descriptions Act 1968

11. In section 2(5) of the Trade Descriptions Act 1968, for " Food and Drugs Act 1955 " substitute " Food Act 1984 ".

12. In section 22(2) of that Act—

(*a*) for " Food and Drugs Act 1955 " substitute " Food Act 1984 " ;

(*b*) in paragraph (*a*) of that subsection, for " said Act of 1955, sections 93 and 97 " substitute " said Act of 1984, sections 80 and 84 " ;

(*c*) for " section 123 or 123A of the said Act of 1955 " substitute " section 118 or 119 of the said Act of 1984 ".

Health Services and Public Health Act 1968

13. In section 62 of the Health Services and Public Health Act 1968—

(*a*) in subsection (1)—

(i) omit " and in the Food and Drugs Act 1955 references to ships ", and

(ii) for " in each of those Acts " substitute " in that Act " ;

(*b*) in subsection (2) for " for the references therein to the Public Health Act 1936 and the Food and Drugs Act 1955, there were substituted references respectively to " substitute " the reference to the Public Health Act 1936 included references to both ".

Medicines Act 1968

14. In section 132(1) of the Medicines Act 1968, in the definition of " food and drugs authority ", for " Food and Drugs Act 1955 by section 198 of the Local Government Act 1972 " substitute " Food Act 1984 by section 71 of that Act ".

15. In paragraph 1(2) of Schedule 3 to that Act, for " section 89(1) of the Food and Drugs Act 1955 " substitute " section 76(1) of the Food Act 1984 ".

Transport Act 1968

16. In paragraph 7(2)(*d*) of Schedule 16 to the Transport Act 1968, for " section 11(2) of the Food and Drugs Act 1955 " substitute " section 11(4) of the Food Act 1984 ".

Agriculture Act 1970

17. In subsections (4) and (5) of section 25 of the Agriculture Act 1970, for " Food and Drugs Act 1955 " substitute " Food Act 1984 ".

Tribunals and Inquiries Act 1971

18. In paragraph 15 of Part I of Schedule 1 to the Tribunals and Inquiries Act 1971, for " Food and Drugs Act 1955 (c.16) " substitute " Food Act 1984 ".

Road Traffic Act 1972

1972 c. 20.
1955 c. 16
(4 & 5 Eliz. 2).

19. In section 10(7) of the Road Traffic Act 1972, for " section 89 of the Food and Drugs Act 1955 " substitute " section 76 of the Food Act 1984 ".

1972 c. xl.

Greater London Council (General Powers) Act 1972

20. In paragraph (*a*) of section 17(5) of the Greater London Council (General Powers) Act 1972, for " Food and Drugs Act, 1955 " substitute " Food Act 1984, other than Part IV ".

1972 c. 66.

Poisons Act 1972

21. In paragraph (*a*) of section 8(4) of the Poisons Act 1972, for " section 89 of the Food and Drugs Act 1955 " substitute " section 76 of the Food Act 1984 ".

1972 c. 70.

Local Government Act 1972

22. In section 112(4) of the Local Government Act 1972, for " section 89 of the Food and Drugs Act 1955 " substitute " section 76 of the Food Act 1984 ".

23. In section 259(3) of that Act—

    (*a*) in paragraph (*b*) for " Food and Drugs Act 1955 " substitute " Food Act 1984 " ;

    (*b*) for paragraph (*c*) substitute—

1936 c. 49.
1974 c. 3.

        " (*c*) any transfer or relinquishment of functions under any of the provisions of the Public Health Act 1936—

            (i) which are incorporated in the Slaughterhouses Act 1974 ; or

            (ii) which are repealed by the Food Act 1984 to the extent that those provisions were incorporated in the Food and Drugs Act 1955, and which are reproduced in that Act of 1984 ; ".

1973 c. xxx.

Greater London Council (General Powers) Act 1973

24. In section 2 of the Greater London Council (General Powers) Act 1973, for " ' the Act of 1955 ' means the Food and Drugs Act 1955 " substitute " ' the Act of 1984 ' means the Food Act 1984 ".

25. In subsections (1) and (9) of section 30 of that Act, for " Act of 1955 " substitute " Act of 1984 ".

26. In section 32(3) of that Act, for " subsection (5) of section 100 of the Act of 1955 " substitute " section 87(5) of the Act of 1984 ".

1973 c. 32.

National Health Service Reorganisation Act 1973

27. In paragraph (*a*) (ii) of section 18(3) of the National Health Service Reorganisation Act 1973, for " Food and Drugs Act 1955 " substitute " Food Act 1984 ".

Slaughterhouses Act 1974

28. In the Slaughterhouses Act 1974—

    (*a*) in paragraph (*a*) of section 2(2),

    (*b*) in paragraph (*a*) of section 4(2),

    (*c*) in section 12(2),

    (*d*) in section 16(3),

for " Food and Drugs Act 1955 " substitute " Food Act 1984 ".

Weights and Measures etc. Act 1976

29. In section 12 of the Weights and Measures Act 1976—

    (*a*) in subsection (1)(*a*), for "Food and Drugs Act 1955 (the '1955 Act')" substitute "Food Act 1984 (the '1984 Act')";

    (*b*) in subsection (9)(*a*), for " the 1955 Act " substitute " the 1984 Act ".

30. In paragraph 2 of Schedule 6 to that Act—

    (*a*) in sub-paragraph (1), for " Food and Drugs Act 1955 " substitute " Food Act 1984 ";

    (*b*) in sub-paragraph (2)—

        (i) for " Part V " substitute " Part VI ";

        (ii) for "sections 126, 127, 128 and 131 " substitute " sections 109, 111, 112, 113(1)-(4), sections 114 to 117, sections 122 to 125, sections 127 to 130, section 132(2) and Schedule 9 paragraph 3(1) and (2) ".

City of London (Various Powers) Act 1977

31. In section 22(2) of the City of London (Various Powers) Act 1977—

    (*a*) for " section 100 of the Food and Drugs Act 1955 " substitute " section 87 of the Food Act 1984 "; and

    (*b*) for " section 101(2) " substitute " section 88(2) ".

Consumer Safety Act 1978

32. In the Consumer Safety Act 1978—

    (*a*) in paragraph (*b*) of the definition of "goods " in section 9(4), and

    (*b*) in paragraph (*g*) (i) of section 11,

for " section 135(1) of the Food and Drugs Act 1955 " substitute " section 131(1) of the Food Act 1984 ".

Hydrocarbon Oil Duties Act 1979

33. In paragraph 5(*d*) of Schedule 5 to the Hydrocarbon Oil Duties Act 1979, for " section 89 of the Food and Drugs Act 1955 " substitute " section 76 of the Food Act 1984 ".

Sch. 10
1982 c. 30.

1955 c. 16
(4 & 5 Eliz. 2).

1984 c. 22.

Section 134.

Local Government (Miscellaneous Provisions) Act 1982

34. In paragraph 11(*b*) of Schedule 4 to the Local Government (Miscellaneous Provisions) Act 1982, for " section 55 of the Food and Drugs Act 1955 " substitute " section 56 of the Food Act 1984 ".

Public Health (Control of Disease) Act 1984

35. In paragraph (*a*) of section 3(2) of the Public Health (Control of Disease) Act 1984, for " Food and Drugs Act 1955 " substitute " Food Act 1984 ".

36. In paragraph (*d*) of section 7(3) of that Act, for " Food and Drugs Act 1955 " substitute " Food Act 1984, other than Part IV ".

37. In paragraph (*b*) of section 20(1) of that Act, for " section 23 of the Food and Drugs Act 1955 " substitute " section 28 of the Food Act 1984 ".

SCHEDULE 11

Repeals and Revocations

Acts

Chapter	Short title	Extent of repeal
4 & 5 Eliz. 2. c. 16.	Food and Drugs Act 1955.	The whole Act.
4 & 5 Eliz. 2. c. 48.	Sugar Act 1956.	The whole Act.
10 & 11 Eliz. 2. c. 46.	Transport Act 1962.	In Part I of Schedule 2, the entry relating to the Food and Drugs Act 1955.
1963 c. 33.	London Government Act 1963.	Section 54(4). In Schedule 13, Part II.
1967 c. 80.	Criminal Justice Act 1967.	In Part I of Schedule 3, the entry relating to the Food and Drugs Act 1955.
1968 c. 46.	Health Services and Public Health Act 1968.	In section 62(1), the words " and in the Food and Drugs Act 1955 references to ships "
1970 c. 3.	Food and Drugs (Milk) Act 1970.	The whole Act.
1971 c. 23.	Courts Act 1971.	In Part I of Schedule 9, the entry relating to the Food and Drugs Act 1955.
1972 c. 68.	European Communities Act 1972.	Section 7(3), (4). In Schedule 4, paragraph 3.
1972 c. 70.	Local Government Act 1972.	Sections 198 and 199.
1973 c. 32.	National Health Service Reorganisation Act 1973.	In paragraph 123 of Schedule 4, the words " and references to ships in the Food and Drugs Act 1955 ".
1974 c. 3.	Slaughterhouses Act 1974.	Section 46(2). In Schedule 3, paragraph 1. Schedule 4.

Chapter	Short title	Extent of repeal
1974 c. 7.	Local Government Act 1974.	In Schedule 6, paragraph 11.
1976 c. 37.	Food and Drugs (Control of Food Premises) Act 1976.	The whole Act.
1977 c. 45.	Criminal Law Act 1977.	In Schedule 6, the entry relating to the Food and Drugs Act 1955.
1979 c. 2.	Customs and Excise Management Act 1979.	In paragraph 12 of Schedule 4, in Part I of the Table, the entry relating to the Food and Drugs Act 1955.
1980 c. 43.	Magistrates' Courts Act 1980.	In Schedule 7, paragraphs 14 and 15.
1980 c. 65.	Local Government, Planning and Land Act 1980.	In Schedule 1, paragraphs 6 and 7.
1981 c. 22.	Animal Health Act 1981.	In Schedule 5, paragraph 2.
1981 c. 26.	Food and Drugs (Amendment) Act 1981.	The whole Act.
1981 c. 67.	Acquisition of Land Act 1981.	In paragraph 1 of Schedule 4, the entry in the Table relating to the Food and Drugs Act 1955.
1982 c. 26.	Food and Drugs (Amendment) Act 1982.	The whole Act.
1982 c. 30.	Local Government (Miscellaneous Provisions) Act 1982.	Part IX.
1982 c. 48.	Criminal Justice Act 1982.	In Schedule 3, the entry relating to the Food and Drugs Act 1955.
1983 c. 41.	Health and Social Services and Social Security Adjudications Act 1983.	Paragraph (a) of section 27.

ORDERS

Year and number	Title	Extent of revocation
S.I. 1966/1305.	London Government Order 1966.	Article 2(11).
S.I. 1968/1699	Secretary of State for Social Services Order 1968.	In Part I of the Schedule, the entry relating to the Food and Drugs Act 1955.
S.I. 1973/2095.	Local Government Re-organisation (Consequential Provisions) (Northern Ireland) Order 1973.	In Schedule 1, paragraph 5.
S.I. 1978/272.	Transfer of Functions (Wales) (No. 1) Order 1978.	In Schedule 5, paragraphs 6 and 7.

TABLE OF DERIVATIONS

Notes—1. The following abbreviations are used in this Table—

1936	= Public Health Act 1936 c. 49.
1955	= Food and Drugs Act 1955 (4 & 5 Eliz. 2) c. 16.
1956	= Sugar Act 1956 c. 48.
1962	= Transport Act 1962 c. 46.
1963	= London Government Act 1963 c. 33.
1968	= Transport Act 1968 c. 73.
1969	= Transport (London) Act 1969 c. 35.
1970	= Food and Drugs (Milk) Act 1970 c. 3.
1972	= European Communities Act 1972 c. 68.
1972 c. 70	= Local Government Act 1972 c. 70.
1974	= Slaughterhouses Act 1974 c. 3.
1976	= Food and Drugs (Control of Food Premises) Act 1976 c. 37.
1976 c. 57	= Local Government (Miscellaneous Provisions) Act 1976 c. 57.
1977	= Criminal Law Act 1977 c. 45.
1979	= Customs and Excise Management Act 1979 c. 2.
1980	= Magistrates' Courts Act 1980 c. 43.
1981	= Animal Health Act 1981 c. 22.
1981 c. 26	= Food and Drugs (Amendment) Act 1981 c. 26.
1981 c. 67	= Acquisition of Land Act 1981 c. 67.
1982	= Food and Drugs (Amendment) Act 1982 c. 26.
1982 c. 30	= Local Government (Miscellaneous Provisions) Act 1982 c. 30.
1982 c. 48	= Criminal Justice Act 1982 c. 48.

2. The Table does not generally acknowledge transfers of ministerial functions.

Provision	Derivation
1(1)	1955 s. 1(1), (4).
(2)	1955 s. 1(3), (4).
(3)	1955 s. 1(6).
(4)	1955 s. 1(5).
2(1)	1955 s. 2(1).
(2)	1955 s. 2(2), (3).
3(1)	1955 s. 3(1).
(2)	1955 s. 3(3).
(3)	1955 s. 3(4); Council Directive No. 76/766/EEC (O.J. No. L. 262, 27.9.76 p. 149).

Provision	Derivation
4(1)	1955 s. 4(1), Sch. 10 paras. 1, 2 Table; 1972 Sch. 4 para. 3(1).
(2), (3)	1955 s. 4(2), (3).
(4)	1955 s. 4(4), Sch. 10 paras. 1, 2 Table.
(5)	1955 Sch. 10 para. 1.
5(1)–(4)	1955 s. 5(1)–(4).
(5)	1955 Sch. 10 paras. 1, 2 Table.
6(1)–(6)	1955 s. 6(1)–(6).
7(1)	1955 s. 7(1).
(2)	1955 s. 7(3), (4).
(3)	1955 Sch. 10 para. 1.
8(1)–(3)	1955 s. 8(1)–(3).
(4)	1955 s. 8(4); 1974 Sch. 3 para. 1.
(5)	1955 s. 8(5).
9(1)–(4)	1955 s. 9(1)–(4).
10	1955 s. 10(1), (2).
11(1)–(3)	1955 s. 11(1).
(4)	1955 s. 11(2); 1962 Sch. 2 Pt. I; 1968 s. 60 Sch. 16 para. 7; 1969 Sch. 3 para. 1.
(5)	1955 s. 11(3).
12(1)	1955 s. 12(1).
(2)	1955 s. 12(2); 1974 Sch. 3 para. 1.
13(1)	1955 s. 13(1).
(2)	1955 s. 13(2), (3).
(3)	1955 s. 13(4).
(4), (5)	1955 s. 13(5).
(6)–(8)	1955 s. 13(6)–(8).
(9)	1955 s. 13(9); 1974 Sch. 4 para. 1.
(10)	1955 Sch. 10 para. 1.
14(1)	1955 s. 14(1).
(2), (3)	1955 s. 14(2).
(4)	1955 s. 14(3).
(5)	1955 s. 14(4), (5).
(6)	1955 s. 14(4).
(7)	1955 s. 14(6).
15	1955 s. 15(1).
16(1), (2)	1955 s. 16(1), (2).
(3)	1955 s. 16(3), (3A); 1981 c. 26 s. 1.
(4), (5)	1955 s. 16(4), (5).
(6), (7)	1955 s. 20.
17(1), (2)	1955 s. 17(1), (2).
(3), (4)	1955 s. 17(3).
(5)	1955 s. 17(4).
(6), (7)	1955 s. 20.
18(1)–(3)	1955 s. 18(1)–(3).
(4)	1955 s. 18(4); Criminal Justice Act 1967 c. 80 Sch. 3; 1982 c. 48 ss. 38, 46.
19(1), (2)	1955 s. 19(1).
(3)	1955 s. 19(2).
(4)	1955 s. 19(3).
(5)	1955 s. 19(4).

Provision	Derivation
20(1)–(5)	1955 s. 21(1)–(5).
21(1)–(4)	1976 s. 1(1)–(4).
22(1)–(6)	1976 s. 2(1)–(6).
23(1), (2)	1976 s. 3(1), (2).
24(1)–(3)	1976 s. 4(1)–(3).
25(1) (2)	1976 s. 5(1); 1982 c. 48 ss. 38, 46. 1976 s. 6(1).
26	1976 s. 7(1)–(3).
27(1) (2), (3)	1955 s. 22(1); Criminal Justice Act 1967 c. 80 Sch. 3; 1982 c. 48 ss. 38, 46. 1955 s. 22(2), (3).
28(1) (2) (3) (4), (5) (6)	1955 s. 23(1); Criminal Justice Act 1967 c. 80 Sch. 3; 1972 c. 70 s. 199(1); 1982 ss. 38, 46. 1955 s. 23(2). 1955 s. 23(3); 1967 c. 80 Sch. 3; 1972 c. 70 Sch. 29 para. 4(1); 1982 c. 48 ss. 39, 46, Sch. 3. 1955 s. 23(4), (5); 1972 c. 70 Sch. 29 para. 4(1). 1955 s. 23(5).
29(1) (2) (3) (4)	1955 s. 24(1), (3). 1955 s. 24(2), (3). 1955 s. 24(4). 1955 s. 24(5).
30(1)–(3) (4) (5)	1955 s. 25(1)–(3). 1955 s. 25(5). 1955 s. 25(6).
31(1) (2), (3)	1955 s. 27(1); 1972 c. 70 Sch. 29 para. 4(1); 1982 c. 48 ss. 39, 46, Sch. 3. 1955 s. 27(2), (3); 1972 c. 70 Sch. 29 para. 4(1).
32(1), (2)	1955 s. 28(1), (2).
33(1)–(4)	1955 s. 29(1)–(4).
34(1)–(5)	1955 s. 30(1)–(5).
35(1) (2) (3)	1955 s. 31(1), (3). 1955 s. 31(2). 1955 s. 31(4).
36(1) (2), (3) (4)	1955 s. 32(1), (3)–(5). 1955 s. 32(6). 1955 s. 32(7); 1970 s. 1(1).
37	1955 s. 34.
38(1) (2) (3), (4)	1955 s. 35(1). 1955 s. 35(2); 1972 c. 70 s. 199(2). 1955 s. 35(3), (4).
39(1) (2) (3)	1955 s. 36(1), (3). 1955 s. 36(2), (3). 1955 s. 36(4).

Provision	Derivation
39(4)	1955 s. 36(5).
(5)	1955 s. 36(6).
40(1)–(6)	1955 s. 37(1)–(6).
41(1)–(3)	1955 s. 38(1)–(3).
(4), (5)	1955 s. 38(4).
(6)	1955 s. 37(6).
42(1)–(3)	1955 s. 39(1)–(3).
(4)	1955 s. 37(6).
43(1)	1955 s. 41(2).
(2)	1955 s. 41(3).
(3)	1955 s. 41(4).
(4)	1955 s. 45.
(5)	1955 s. 37(6).
44(1)–(3)	1955 ss. 42(1)–(3).
(4)	1955 ss. 37(6), 42(4); 1972 c. 70 s. 272(2).
45(1)–(3)	1955 s. 43(1)–(3).
(4)	1955 ss. 37(6), 43(4); 1972 c. 70 s. 272(2).
46(1)–(3)	1955 s. 44(1)–(3).
(4)	1955 s. 37(6).
47	1955 s. 46.
48(1)	1955 s. 47(1), (5).
(2)–(4)	1955 s. 47(2)–(4).
49	1955 s. 48.
50(1)	1955 s. 49(1); 1972 c. 70 s. 199(3).
(2), (3)	1955 s. 49(3).
51(1), (2)	1955 s. 50.
52	1955 s. 51.
53(1)	1955 s. 52(1).
(2)	1955 s. 52(2); 1972 c. 70 s. 199(4).
(3)	1955 s. 52(3).
(4)	1955 s. 52(4); 1982 c. 48 ss. 39, 46, Sch. 3.
(5)	1955 s. 52(5).
54(1)–(3)	1955 s. 53(1)–(3).
55	1955 s. 54(1), (2).
56(1)	1955 s. 55(1); 1977 Sch. 6; 1982 c. 48 s. 46.
(2)	1955 s. 55(2).
57(1), (2)	1955 s. 56(1), (2).
58	1955 s. 57(1), 1982 c. 48 ss. 39, 46, Sch. 3.
59	1955 s. 58.
60	1955 s. 61.

Provision	Derivation
61	1955 ss. 49(2), 52(1), 53(4), 135(1), 137(3); 1963 Sch. 13 para. 4; S.I. 1966/1305 art. 2(11).
62	1982 c. 30 s. 18(1).
63	1982 c. 30 s. 18(2)–(4).
64(1)	1982 c. 30 s. 19(1), (3).
(2)	1982 c. 30 s. 19(2).
65(1)	1982 c. 30 s. 19(4); 1982 c. 48 ss. 37, 46.
(2)	1982 c. 30 s. 19(5).
66(1)	1982 c. 30 s. 19(6).
(2)	1982 c. 30 s. 19(7).
(3)	1982 c. 30 s. 19(8).
(4)	1982 c. 30 s. 19(9).
(5)	1982 c. 30 s. 19(10).
67(1)	1982 c. 30 s. 19(12).
(2)	1982 c. 30 s. 18(5).
(3)	1982 c. 30 s. 19(11), (12).
68(1), (2)	1956 s. 18(1), (2).
(3), (4)	1956 s. 18(5).
(5)	1956 s. 18(6).
(6)	1956 ss. 18(9), 23(4), 35(2); S.I. 1978/272 Sch. 5 para. 7.
69(1), (2)	1972 s. 7(3).
(3)	1956 s. 35(2); 1972 s. 7(4).
70(1)	1955 s. 80(1).
(2), (3)	1955 s. 80(2).
(4)	1955 s. 80(4); 1974 Sch. 4 para. 2.
71	1972 c. 70 s. 198(1), (2).
72	1955 s. 85; 1972 c. 70 s. 199(5); 1976 s. 6(2).
73(1)	1955 s. 86(1).
(2)	1955 s. 86(4).
74(1)–(3)	1955 s. 87(1)–(3).
(4)	1955 Sch. 10 paras. 1, 2 Table; S.I. 1973/2095 Sch. 1 para. 5.
75	1955 s. 88(2).
76(1), (2)	1955 s. 89(1), (2).
(3)	1955 s. 89(4).
(4)	1955 s. 89(5).
77	1955 s. 90.
78(1)–(8)	1955 s. 91(1)–(8).
79(1)–(6)	1955 s. 92(1)–(6).
80(1)–(3)	1955 s. 93(1)–(3).
(4)	1955 s. 93(4); Decimal Currency Act 1969 c. 19 c. 10(1).
81(1)	1955 s. 94(1).
(2)	1955 s. 94(2); 1972 c. 70 Sch. 29 para. 4(1).
(3), (4)	1955 s. 94(3), (4).

Provision	Derivation
82	1955 s. 95.
83(1), (2)	1955 s. 96(1), (2).
84	1955 s. 97.
85	1955 s. 98.
86	1955 s. 99.
87(1)–(4) (5) (6)	1955 s. 100(1)–(4). 1955 s. 100(5); 1982 c. 48 ss. 38, 46. 1955 s. 100(6); 1981 Sch. 5, para. 2.
88(1), (2)	1955 s. 101(1), (2).
89(1), (2) (3)	1955 s. 103(1), (2). 1955 s. 103(3); 1974 Sch. 4 para. 3.
90(1)–(3)	1955 s. 104(1)–(3).
91(1) (2) (3) (4)	1955 s. 105(1); 1982 c. 48 ss. 39, 46, Sch. 3. 1955 s. 105(2). 1955 ss. 104(3), 105(3); 1982 c. 48 ss. 39, 46, Sch. 3. 1955 s. 105(4).
92(1) (2)	1955 s. 106(1); 1982 s. 1. 1955 ss. 5(3), 106(2); 1982 s. 1.
93(1)–(3) (4)	1955 s. 106A(1)–(3); 1982 s. 2. 1955 Sch. 10 para. 1; 1982 s. 8(1).
94(1), (2)	1955 s. 107(1), (2).
95(1) (2), (3) (4) (5) (6) (7) (8)	1955 s. 108(1); 1982 s. 3. 1955 s. 108(1A); 1982 s. 3. 1955 s. 108(2). 1955 s. 108(3). 1955 s. 108(4). 1955 Sch. 10 para. 3. 1982 s. 10.
96(1) (2)	1955 s. 109(1). 1955 s. 109(2); 1972 c. 70 s. 199(8).
97(1)–(4) (5)	1955 s. 110(1)–(4). 1955 Sch. 10 paras. 1, 2, Table.
98	1955 s. 111.
99(1)–(3)	1955 s. 112(1)–(3).
100(1)–(3)	1955 s. 113(1)–(3); 1976 s. 5(2).
101(1)–(4)	1955 s. 114(1)–(4).
102(1)–(5)	1955 s. 115(1)–(5).
103(1)–(3)	1955 s. 116(1)–(3).
104(1) (2), (3)	1955 s. 117(1); 1976 s. 4(4); 1980 Sch. 7 para. 15. 1955 s. 117(2), (3).

Provision	Derivation
105	1955 s. 118; Courts Act 1971 c. 23 Sch. 9 Pt. I.
106	1955 s. 119.
107(1), (2)	1955 s. 120(1), (2).
108	1955 s. 121.
109	1936 s. 303; 1955 s. 131(1) Sch. 9 Pt. I.
110	1936 s. 343(1); 1955 s. 130(1)–(3); 1981 c. 67 Sch. 4 para. 1 Table.
111	1936 ss. 289, 343(1); 1955 s. 131(1) Sch. 9 Pt. I.
112	1936 s. 318; 1955 s. 131(1) Sch. 9 Pt. L
113(1)–(3) (4) (5)	1936 s. 322(1)–(3); 1955 s. 131(1) Sch. 9 Pt. I. 1936 s. 325; 1955 s. 131(1) Sch. 9 Pt. I. 1955 s. 131(1) Sch. 9 Pt. I.
114	1955 s. 127(1), (3).
115(1), (2) (3)	1936 s. 324(1); 1955 ss. 127(2), 131(1) Sch. 9 Pt. I. 1936 s. 324(2); 1955 ss. 127(2), 131(1) Sch. 9 Pt. I.
116(1), (2) (3) (4)	1955 s. 128(1). 1955 s. 128(2). 1955 s. 128(3).
117	1936 s. 304; 1955 s. 131(1) Sch. 9 Pt. I.
118(1) (2) (3), (4) (5) (6) (7)	1955 s. 123(1); 1982 s. 4(1); 1982 c. 48 s. 46. 1955 s. 123(2); 1982 s. 4(2). 1955 s. 123(3), (4). 1955 s. 123(4A); 1974 Sch. 4 para. 4. 1955 s. 123(6). 1955 Sch. 10 paras. 1, 2 Table.
119(1), (2)	1955 s. 123A(1), (2); 1972 Sch. 4 para. 3(2).
120(1) (2) (3) (4) (5)	1955 s. 124(1); 1956 s. 33(1); Agriculture Act 1967 c. 22 s. 4(2); 1976 s. 7(4). 1955 s. 124(2); 1956 s. 33(2); 1972 Sch. 4 para. 3(2); 1976 s. 7(4). 1955 s. 124(3). 1955 s. 124(4). 1955 Sch. 10 paras. 1, 2 Table.
121(1) (2) (3)	1955 s. 125(1). 1955 s. 125(3). 1955 s. 125(4).
122	1936 s. 283(1); 1955 s. 131(1) Sch. 9 Pt. I.
123	1936 s. 283(2); 1955 s. 131(1) Sch. 9 Pt. I.
124(1) (2)	1936 s. 284(1); 1955 s. 131(1) Sch. 9 Pt. I; 1972 c. 70 Sch. 29 Pt. I para. 4. 1936 s. 284(2); 1955 s. 131(1) Sch. 9 Pt. I.
125	1936 s. 285; 1955 s. 131(1) Sch. 9 Pt. I; 1972 c. 70 s. 29 Pt. I para. 4.
126	1955 s. 132.
127	1955 s. 126(1A); 1974 Sch. 4 para. 5.

Provision	Derivation
128	1955 s. 126(2).
129(1)	1955 s. 126(4); 1972 c. 70 s. 179(3).
(2)	1955 s. 126(5).
(3)	1955 s. 126(7); 1972 c. 70 s. 179(3).
130(1), (2)	1955 s. 126(6).
131(1), (2)	1955 s. 135(1), (2).
132(1)	1955 s. 135(1); 1956 s. 17(1); 1963 Sch. 13 para. 3; Health Services and Public Health Act 1968 c. 46 s. 62(1); 1972 c. 70 s. 270(3); National Health Service Reorganisation Act 1973 c. 32 Sch. 4 para. 123; 1976 ss. 1, 2; S.I. 1978/272 Sch. 5 para. 6; 1979 Sch. 4 para. 12; 1982 s. 9; 1982 c. 48 s. 75.
(2)	1936 s. 328; 1955 s. 131(1) Sch. 9 Pt. I.
133(1), (2)	1955 s. 122(1), (2).
(3)	1955 Sch. 10 paras. 1, 2 Table.
134	[Transitional and saving provisions; amendments and repeals.]
135(1)	1955 Sch. 10 paras. 1, 2.
(2)	1955 Sch. 10 para. 2; S.I. 1968/1699 Sch. Pt. I; S.I. 1973/2095 Sch. 1 para. 5.
(3)	1955 Sch. 10 para. 5.
136(1)	[Citation].
(2)	1955 s. 137(4); 1956 s. 36; 1970 s. 2; 1972 s. 7(4); 1976 s. 8(3); 1981 c. 26 s. 2(2); 1982 s. 11; 1982 c. 30 s. 49(2).
(3)	1955 s. 137(5); 1956 s. 36(3); 1970 s. 2(2); 1972 s. 7(4); 1976 s. 8(3); 1981 c. 26 s. 2(2); 1982 ss. 8, 11; 1982 c. 30 s. 49(2).
(4)	[Commencement].
Schedules 1–5	1955 Schedules 1–5.
Sch. 6	1955 Sch. 6; 1972 c. 70 s. 199(9).
Sch. 7 paras. 1–9	1955 Sch. 7 paras. 1–9.
10	1955 Sch. 7 para. 10; Recorded Delivery Service Act 1962 c. 27 s. 1(1).
11–17	1955 Sch. 7 paras. 11–17.
Sch. 8	1955 Sch. 8.
Sch. 9 para. 1	[Drafting provision.]
2	1955 s. 41(1).
3(1)	1936 s. 317; 1955 s. 131(1) Sch. 9 Pt. I.
(2)	1955 s. 131(2) Sch. 9 Pt. II.
(3)	[Drafting provision.]
4, 5	[Drafting provisions.]
6(1)	1956 s. 23(4).
(2)	1956 s. 22.
7	[Drafting provision.]
Sch. 10	[Consequential amendments.]
Sch. 11	[Repeals and revocations.]

Printed in the United Kingdom for HMSO
Dd 5060569   12/92   C4   35335   ON 226133

PRINTED IN ENGLAND BY PAUL FREEMAN
Controller and Chief Executive of Her Majesty's Stationery Office and
Queen's Printer of Acts of Parliament.

4th Impression July 1984

6th Impression December 1992